The Very Easy Guide to
Fair Isle Knitting

The Very Easy Guide to
Fair Isle Knitting

Step-by-Step Techniques, Easy-to-Follow Stitch Patterns, and Projects to Get You Started

Lynne Watterson

St. Martin's Griffin
New York

Library of Congress Cataloging-in-Publication
Data Available Upon Request

ISBN 978-1-250-01622-5

QUAR.GFK

Conceived, designed, and produced by
Quarto Publishing plc
The Old Brewery
6 Blundell Street
London N7 9BH

Project Editor: Chloe Todd Fordham
Illustrator: Kuo Kang Chen
Photographer: Phil Wilkins
Project Photographer: Lizzie Orme
Designer: Tanya Goldsmith
Art Director: Caroline Guest
Creative Director: Moira Clinch
Publisher: Paul Carslake

Color reproduction by
Modern Age Repro House Ltd, Singapore
Printed in China by
Hung Hing Off-set Printing Co. Ltd

First U.S. Edition December 2012

10 9 8 7 6 5 4 3 2 1

contents

introduction

Knitting Fair Isle isn't as difficult as it looks and with this book I will guide you through the techniques so that you can enjoy knitting beautiful Fair Isle patterns as much as I do.

So often knitters are put off by the number of colors used in a Fair Isle pattern. Although several colors may make up the pattern, traditionally no more than two colors are used in a row. Therefore, it is only a matter of learning how to work with two colors at a time.

The Fair Isle patterns are divided into four lessons: Corrugated ribbing, Seeding, Fair Isle bands, and Fair Isle patterns. Each lesson features stunning Fair Isle patterns in beautiful color combinations. You can mix and match the patterns from each lesson to produce your own fabrics. The stitch patterns can be used to practice Fair Isle techniques, design your own projects, or to substitute the stitch patterns used for the projects in this book—just remember to check the gauge carefully if you are substituting a pattern.

To complete each lesson, a collection of simple stunning projects has been designed using a selection of the stitch patterns. The projects will give you a chance to practice knitting Fair Isle on two needles, four needles, and circular needles.

I hope you enjoy this form of color knitting. I find it so exciting to plan the design and then watch the patterns grow on my knitted fabric—I hope you do too!

This book is dedicated to my sister Christina. Thank you for letting me take over your beautiful home to shoot the projects. With my love always.

about this book

This book guides you through the entire process of Fair Isle knitting, from the very basics of knitting, through the different stitches and patterns, to making projects with the perfect finish.

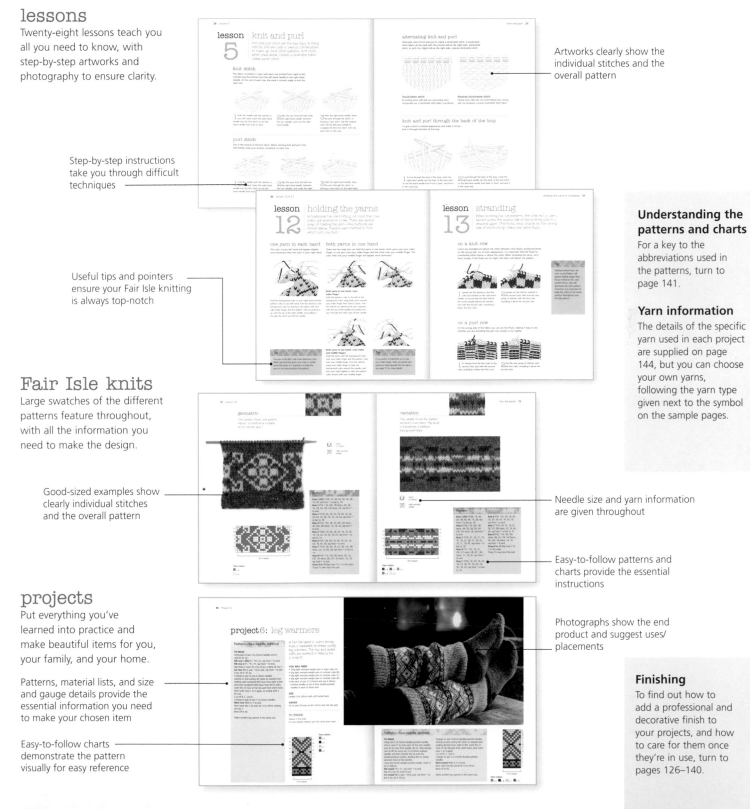

lessons

Twenty-eight lessons teach you all you need to know, with step-by-step artworks and photography to ensure clarity.

Artworks clearly show the individual stitches and the overall pattern

Step-by-step instructions take you through difficult techniques

Useful tips and pointers ensure your Fair Isle knitting is always top-notch

Fair Isle knits

Large swatches of the different patterns feature throughout, with all the information you need to make the design.

Good-sized examples show clearly individual stitches and the overall pattern

projects

Put everything you've learned into practice and make beautiful items for you, your family, and your home.

Patterns, material lists, and size and gauge details provide the essential information you need to make your chosen item

Easy-to-follow charts demonstrate the pattern visually for easy reference

Understanding the patterns and charts

For a key to the abbreviations used in the patterns, turn to page 141.

Yarn information

The details of the specific yarn used in each project are supplied on page 144, but you can choose your own yarns, following the yarn type given next to the symbol on the sample pages.

Needle size and yarn information are given throughout

Easy-to-follow patterns and charts provide the essential instructions

Photographs show the end product and suggest uses/placements

Finishing

To find out how to add a professional and decorative finish to your projects, and how to care for them once they're in use, turn to pages 126–140.

lesson
1
yarns

Knitting yarns are usually produced by spinning fibers together. Traditionalists favor Shetland wool for Fair Isle, although cotton, wool and alpaca mixes, and novelty yarns can be used too.

Wool is the yarn most commonly associated with knitting. Spun from the fleece of sheep, it has many excellent qualities—durability, elasticity, and warmth. It is available in different plies and a wide range of colors, as well as 100 percent undyed virgin wool.

Shetland wool is spun from the fleece of the native Shetland breed of sheep and is perfect for Fair Isle knitting. The fleece is soft and well crimped—the natural crimp helps the floats stay in place. This lightweight wool is available in 11 natural colors, plus a wide variety of dyed colors. The beauty of Shetland wool is shown after washing: a wispy haze appears, muting the color changes.

Tip

Yarns are available in many different weights or thicknesses—from very fine to extra bulky. Your chosen pattern will tell you which weight of yarn is required and the needle sizes to achieve the designer's recommended gauge (number of stitches and rows over a given measurement, see page 26).

Tip

Keep the yarn label as a reference with the gauge swatch in a safe place, together with any leftover yarn and spare buttons. The label can be referred to when washing the item and spare yarn and buttons can be used for repairs.

Space-dyed yarn can be used as the main yarn for a Fair Isle design, with a plain color used for the contrast. By using a space-dyed yarn, a variety of tones can be worked into the design without using several balls of different color yarns. Yarn can be space-dyed in two or more tonal colors—as shown below— or in two or more contrasting colors— shown above. It is available in natural or synthetic fibers; make sure you match the fibers of the main and contrast yarns.

Alpaca is a soft, luxurious fiber from the fleece of the alpaca. It is a strong fiber with excellent thermal properties and is valued for its silky feel and warmth. When mixed with wool it produces a hardwearing fabric with a soft haze.

Cotton is a soft, natural plant fiber that grows around the seeds of the cotton plant. The yarn produced by spinning the fibers is ideal for all seasons—warm in the winter and cool in the summer. Cotton gives a special crispness to Fair Isle patterns, but does tend to be heavy and stranding will add extra weight to the project.

Understanding yarn labels
The band or label attached to yarn gives you important information about the yarn, helping you to make the right choice for your project.
- Company logo (1)
- Yarn name (2)
- Fiber content and place of origin (3)
- Length of yarn in the ball (4)
- Weight of yarn in the ball (5)
- Recommended knitted gauge/ needle size (6)
- Color (7)
- Dye lot (8)
- Care instructions (9)

lesson 2

choosing colors

The great charm of Fair Isle patterns lies in their clever use of color. Most patterns use several colors, and choosing your yarn palette is key to the success of the design. This can be an exciting and stimulating process. It can also be fraught with uncertainty and indecision. A basic understanding of simple color theory provides a good starting point for the selection process.

The colors you choose for a piece of Fair Isle knitting must work together to display the design to its best advantage. It's not always easy to get it right. If the colors are too close in tone, the pattern will not show up—colors change their value according to the colors they are next to. In addition, the colors must work for the wearer—they can enliven skin tones or have an opposite draining effect. With all these considerations there is inevitably a certain amount of trial and error involved in getting the palette exactly right, but a little knowledge takes away some of the guesswork.

the color wheel

Some color partnerships create a harmonious effect that's easy on the eye, while others create vibrant and energetic relationships with stimulating contrasts. The 12 shades on the wheel are described as either "warm" or "cool"—an infinite number of mixes creates a vast array of shades within these two basic color "families." An artist's color wheel helps to explain all these effects.

Primary colors The primary colors in the spectrum are red, yellow, and blue, which cannot be mixed from other colors. All other colors are made by mixing these three pure hues.

Secondary colors The secondary colors are orange (red mixed with yellow), green (yellow mixed with blue), and violet (blue mixed with red). These sit between the primaries on the color wheel.

Complementary colors Complementary colors are those that are directly opposite each other on the wheel. Thus the complementary of green is red, the complementary of yellow is violet, and so on. These contrast sharply with each other and create a lively and eye-catching effect.

Harmonious colors Harmonious colors are those that sit near to each other on the color wheel—the greens and blues, or the oranges and yellows. Working within these groupings creates gently coordinated effects with no startling contrasts.

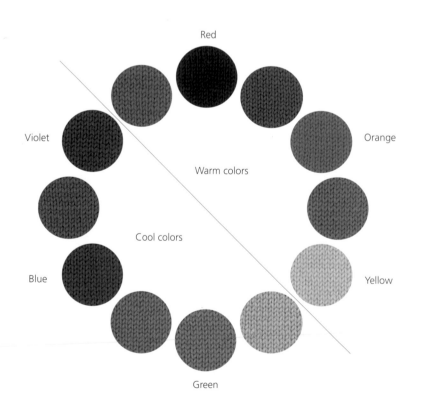

Red

Violet

Warm colors

Orange

Cool colors

Blue

Yellow

Green

choosing a color group

Remember that, in Fair Isle knitting, while only two colors are used in each row, the complete pattern may incorporate four or five colors. Consider the whole palette to make sure it balances. You will need an accent color that stands out from the rest but without drawing too much attention to itself. Remember also that you can choose complementary or harmonious colors within each general color group.

Warm palette The six colors from yellow to red-violet that form one half of the wheel are known as "warm" colors. These have a glowing intensity that needs careful management.

Cool palette The remaining shades on the color wheel from violet to yellow-green are the known as "cool" colors. Used together these tend to give a more restful result than a palette of warm colors.

Pastel palette Pastel shades are typified by the reduced intensity of color that gives them their gentle tones. Within the pastel range you can still work with complementary or harmonious groupings.

Bright palette Primary mixes can be too intense. Bright colors are best softened a little with mixes that create intermediate tones.

Neutral palette A palette of muted grays and soft browns can create an effective vehicle for a Fair Isle pattern. They still have subtle biases toward the "warm" or "cool" spectrum.

Warm palette

Cool palette

Pastel palette

Bright palette

Neutral palette

Changing the emphasis

The choice of yarns is just the beginning of the color design process. Knit some samples to see how the colors react with each other. Change the order in which each is introduced into the pattern; use alternative accent colors; change the background color—the same colors can create surprisingly different effects.

The turquoise stripes stand out on this sample.

The diamond pattern is the main emphasis on this sample.

lesson

knitting kit

Here you will find details of the equipment that will form the basis of your knitting workbox and a selection of other equipment that isn't essential but could be useful as you knit your Fair Isle projects.

Knitting needles

Knitting needles come in a wide range of sizes to suit different weights of yarn and a variety of lengths to suit the number of stitches required for a particular project. They are available in various materials, from rigid aluminum to flexible bamboo. Larger-sized needles are made of plastic to reduce their weight. Wood and bamboo needles are lightweight and flexible and virtually silent when knitting.

Circular knitting needles

Since most Fair Isle knitting is worked in the round you will need circular and double-pointed needles of various sizes and lengths. Circular needles consist of two rigid tips of metal, plastic, wood, or bamboo joined by a thin flexible cord. The long linking cord enables large numbers of working stitches to be stored safely without the risk of dropped stitches. In addition, the weight of the work is distributed evenly along the cord, making heavy pieces easier to handle.

Double-pointed needles

Double-pointed needles are used for knitting in the round when the circumference of the piece of knitting is smaller than 16in (40cm). They are available in aluminum, with bamboo and plastic in some sizes, and in sets of four or five needles.

Pins

Long glass-headed pins or knitting pins with a large head are best suited to knitted fabrics—they are easy to see on the knitting and will not get lost in the fabric.

Tapestry needles

A blunt-ended needle with a large eye is required for sewing seams and weaving in ends. They are available in different sizes to suit different weights of yarn.

Scissors

Use small, sharp scissors to cut yarn. Don't attempt to break the yarn with your fingers as this may result in you cutting your skin.

Stitch holders

These long pins are used for holding groups of stitches until they are required—such as neck stitches and the top of a pocket opening.

Tape measure

These come in various materials, colors, and casings—choose one that has clear numbers and is easy to read.

extras

Graph paper and colored pencils

If you want to design your own Fair Isle patterns, you will find it easy to plan and see your design if you chart on graph paper. Graph paper with 8 or 10 squares to 1in (2.5cm) is a useful size, or you can use a larger-scale graph paper with ¼in (5mm) squares.

Stitch markers

These are available in a variety of styles and sizes—choose a size close to that of your needle. Locking stitch markers are useful for marking the beginning of the round when using circular or double-pointed needles; split ring markers are helpful for marking a particular stitch and stitch repeats.

Row counter

A row counter can be very useful for keeping track of rows or rounds. The barrel type is slipped onto a straight needle and pushed up to the knob. If using large-sized straight needles, you will need the clutch type.

Yarn guide and knitting thimble

These are special tools that sit on the index finger and hold the two colors, keeping them separate and free from tangles. The yarns are held in grooves or metal coils to keep them in a consistent position.

knitting basics

Cast on, bind off, knit, purl, stockinette stitch, reverse stockinette stitch, garter stitch, seed stitch, gauge, and reading charts—simple steps for perfect Fair Isle knitting.

lesson  | casting on

There are several methods of casting on—here we show the thumb method, both English and Continental, and the cable method. These are the most frequently used methods. Unless a pattern states a particular cast on, choose the one you are most comfortable with.

Tip

When you make your slip knot loop, make sure that you leave a long enough end of yarn to cast on the number of stitches required. You need 1yd (1m) of yarn to cast on around 100 stitches in standard weight yarn.

making a slip knot loop

Before you begin your cast on, you first need to make a slip knot loop. This is placed on one needle and is counted as the first stitch.

1 Leaving a long end, wind the yarn from the ball around two fingers of your left hand to form a circle.

2 Use one of your knitting needles to pull a loop of yarn from the ball through the circle.

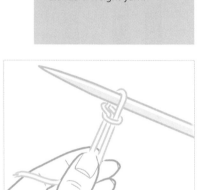

3 Pull both ends of the yarn to tighten the loop on the knitting needle. This loop forms your first stitch.

casting on—thumb method (English)

This method makes a firm, elastic edge that will not stretch out of shape. The yarn is wound around your thumb and each stitch is knitted off your thumb.

1 Make a slip knot loop on one needle. Hold this needle in your right hand. Gripping the loose end of the yarn in the palm of your left hand, wind the yarn clockwise around your thumb.

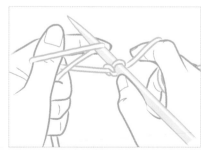

2 Insert the needle into the loop on your thumb from front to back, ready to make the next stitch.

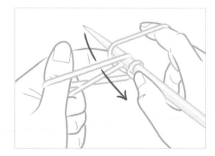

3 Now, take the yarn from the ball under the needle and between the needle and your thumb. Draw the needle through the loop and remove your thumb. Pull the end of yarn to tighten the stitch. Continue to cast on stitches in this way.

casting on—thumb method (Continental)

This method is worked in the same way as the English cast on, except both yarns are held in the left hand. This is favored by knitters who knit in the Continental style.

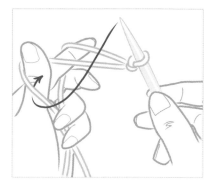

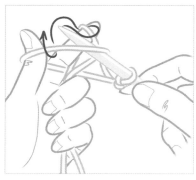

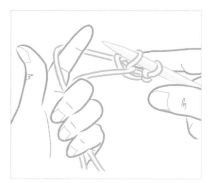

1 Make a slip knot loop on one needle. Hold this needle in your right hand. Take the yarn from the ball over your left index finger and grip it together with the loose end of yarn in the palm of your left hand. Wind the loose end of yarn clockwise around your left thumb.

2 Insert the needle under the yarn across the front of your thumb, then under the yarn across your index finger, and pull a loop through the loop on your thumb.

3 Remove your thumb and pull the ends of the yarn to tighten the stitch. Continue to cast on stitches in this way, making sure the stitches are even and move freely on the needle.

casting on—two-needle method or cable cast on

This is a popular cast on that creates a firm edge. It is worked by knitting a stitch, then transferring it from the right to the left needle.

1 Make a slip knot loop, about 5in (12cm) from the end of the yarn, on one needle. Hold the needle with the slip knot loop in your left hand and insert the right-hand needle into the loop from front to back. Take the yarn from the ball under the right-hand needle and up between the two needles.

2 Draw the right-hand needle back and toward you, pulling the yarn through the slip knot loop to make a new stitch, then transfer the stitch to the left-hand needle.

3 Now insert the right-hand needle between the two stitches on the left-hand needle, and take the yarn under the right-hand needle and up between the needles. Draw a loop through and transfer the new stitch to the left-hand needle. Continue to cast on stitches in this way.

lesson 5 | knit and purl

Knit and purl stitch are the two basic knitting stitches and are used in various combinations to make up most stitch patterns. Knit stitch, when used alone, creates a reversible fabric called garter stitch.

knit stitch

The fabric is knitted in rows, with each row knitted from right to left, transferring the stitches from the left-hand needle to the right-hand needle. At the end of each row, the work is turned, ready to knit the next row.

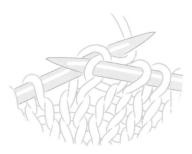

1 Hold the needle with the stitches in your left hand. Insert the right-hand needle into the first stitch on the left-hand needle from front to back.

2 Take the yarn from the ball under the right-hand needle, between the two needles, and over the right-hand needle.

3 With the right-hand needle, draw the yarn through the stitch, so forming a new stitch. Slip the original stitch off the left-hand needle to complete the first knit stitch. Knit into each stitch in this way.

purl stitch

This is the reverse of the knit stitch. When working knit and purl rows alternately, keep the gauge consistent on each row.

1 Hold the needle with the stitches in your left hand. Insert the right-hand needle into the first stitch on the left-hand needle from back to front.

2 Take the yarn from the ball over the right-hand needle, between the two needles, and under the right-hand needle.

3 With the right-hand needle, draw the yarn through the stitch, so forming a new stitch on the right-hand needle. Slip the original stitch off the left-hand needle to complete the first purl stitch. Purl into each stitch in this way to the end of the row.

alternating knit and purl

Alternate rows of knit and purl to create a stockinette stitch. A stockinette stitch fabric can be used with the smooth side as the right side—stockinette stitch; or with the ridged side as the right side—reverse stockinette stitch.

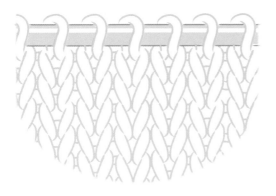

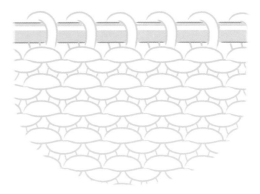

Stockinette stitch

By knitting every right-side row and purling every wrong-side row, a stockinette stitch fabric is produced.

Reverse stockinette stitch

Purling every right-side row and knitting every wrong-side row produces a reverse stockinette stitch fabric.

knit and purl through the back of the loop

To give a stitch a twisted appearance and make it firmer, knit it through the back of the loop.

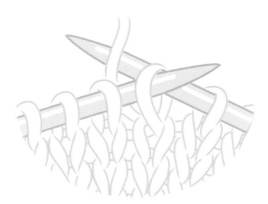

1 To knit through the back of the loop, insert the right-hand needle into the back of the next stitch on the left-hand needle from front to back, and knit it in the usual way.

2 To purl through the back of the loop, insert the right-hand needle into the back of the next stitch on the left-hand needle from back to front, and purl it in the usual way.

lesson 6

reversible fabrics

Reversible knitted fabrics include those made of garter stitch and seed stitch. Both of these stitches work well as textured bands between bands of Fair Isle patterning.

garter stitch

Garter stitch is a simple, reversible fabric that is formed by working every row in knit stitch. It takes a little longer to "grow" than stockinette stitch because two rows show as only one row.

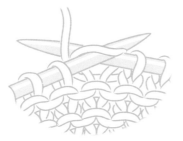

1 Hold the needle with the stitches in your left hand. Use the right-hand needle to knit the first row—"V" stitches are formed on the front of the knitting and ridges on the back.

2 Continue to knit every row in this way to produce a garter stitch fabric.

Tip

This simple stitch is very versatile. When knitted loosely, it's soft and springy. Knitted firmly, on small needles, it is a perfect stitch for bands, borders, and collars.

seed stitch

Seed stitch is another simple stitch to work, and is an ideal fabric to team with Fair Isle. It is produced by knitting and purling alternate stitches across a row, and knitting purl stitches and purling knit stitches on subsequent rows.

1 Cast on an odd number of stitches and hold the needle with the stitches in your left hand. Knit the first stitch, bring the yarn to the front between the needles, and purl the next stitch.

2 Take the yarn to the back and knit the next stitch. Now purl one stitch, then knit one stitch all the way across the row. Each knit stitch will produce a "V" on the front of the fabric, and each purl stitch a ridge.

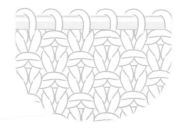

3 On the next row a "V" (knit stitch) is worked over each ridge and a ridge (purl stitch) over each "V." Knit one stitch, then purl one stitch across the row. Continue to work in this way to produce a seed stitch fabric.

lesson

7

binding off

Stitches are bound off to complete your knitting and when a group of stitches is to be decreased—for a buttonhole, an armhole, or a neckline on a garment. When binding off stitches it is important that an even gauge is maintained—neither too tight nor too loose—and that the bind off is elastic. Bind off in the stitch pattern being used, unless stated otherwise.

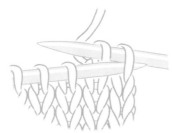

1 When binding off on a knit row, knit the first two stitches so that they are transferred onto the right-hand needle. Insert the left-hand needle, from left to right, into the front of the first stitch on the right-hand needle.

2 Use the left-hand needle to lift the first stitch over the second stitch and off the needle. The first stitch has been bound off and the second stitch remains on the right-hand needle.

3 Knit the next stitch and repeat step 2 to bind off one stitch. Continue to bind off stitches in this way until one stitch remains on the right-hand needle.

4 To secure the last stitch, cut off the yarn about 4in (10cm) from the knitting and draw the end through the last stitch. Pull the end to tighten.

5 When binding off on a purl row, purl the first two stitches so that they are transferred onto the right-hand needle. Insert the left-hand needle, from left to right, into the front of the first stitch on the right-hand needle.

6 Use the left-hand needle to lift the first stitch over the second stitch and off the needle. Continue to bind off stitches in this way and secure the last stitch, as before.

lesson 8 | increasing

To widen a piece of knitting, you will need to add to your stitches by working increases—on a sleeve or to shape a fitted garment, for example. The increases can be made at the beginning or the end of the row, or several invisible increases can be distributed evenly across a row.

increasing a stitch (inc 1)

Single increases are worked by knitting into the front and back of the same stitch.

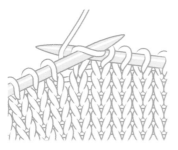

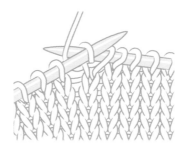

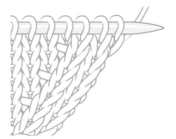

1 Insert the right-hand needle into the front of the next stitch and knit it, but leave it on the left-hand needle.

2 Insert the right-hand needle into the back of the same stitch and work a knit stitch. Slip the original stitch off the left-hand needle. Two stitches have been worked into one stitch.

3 A feature can be made of the shaping by working the increases two or three stitches in from the edge. Here, they are worked two stitches in from the edge and on every knit row.

making a stitch (puk and pup)

Invisible increases are made by working into the loop between two stitches. On a knit row, this is abbreviated as puk; on a purl row, pup.

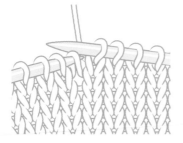

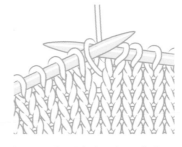

1 Insert the left-hand needle from front to back under the horizontal strand between the last stitch on the right-hand needle and the first stitch on the left-hand needle. This forms a new loop on the left-hand needle.

2 Insert the right-hand needle into the back of this loop, so twisting the loop—this tightens the increase, preventing a hole. Knit into the loop. You will now have one more stitch on the right-hand needle.

Tip

When increasing stitches in a Fair Isle pattern, make sure that you keep the color sequence correct.

lesson 9 | decreasing

To make a piece of knitting narrower, you will need to reduce the number of stitches by working decreases—on a neckline or to shape a hat, for example. As with increasing, decreases can be made at the beginning or end of the row, or distributed evenly across a row.

single decreases

Single decreases are worked over two stitches—knit two together; purl two together; and slip one, knit one, pass slipped stitch over.

knit 2 together (K2 tog)

Insert the right-hand needle into the next two stitches on the left-hand needle and knit the two stitches together.

purl 2 together (P2 tog)

Insert the right-hand needle into the next two stitches on the left-hand needle and purl the two stitches together.

slip 1, knit 1, pass slipped stitch over (skpo)

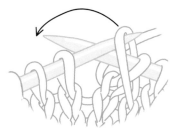

Slip the next stitch, then knit the next stitch. Use the point of the left-hand needle to lift the slipped stitch and pass it over the knit stitch and off the needle.

double decreases

Double decreases are worked over three stitches—slip one, knit two together, pass slipped stitch over; and slip two, knit one, pass two slipped stitches over.

slip 1, knit 2 together, pass slipped stitch over (sl 1, K2 tog, psso)

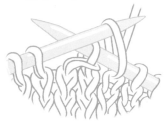

Slip the next stitch, then knit the next two stitches together to decrease a stitch. Use the point of the left-hand needle to lift the slipped stitch and pass it over the knit stitch and off the needle. This slopes to the left on the right side.

slip 2, knit 1, pass 2 slipped stitches over (sl 2, K1, p2sso)

1 Slip the next two stitches from the left-hand needle onto the right-hand needle as if working knit two together.

2 Knit the next stitch, then use the point of the left-hand needle to lift the slipped stitches and pass them over the knit stitch and off the needle to work the double decrease. The decrease sits upright on the right side.

lesson 10

gauge

Before starting any knitting project it is important that you check your gauge—the number of stitches and rows to an inch (or centimeter). The tension achieved by the designer needs to be matched because it determines the measurements of your knitting and ensures that you produce an item that is the correct size and shape.

knitting a gauge swatch

To knit your gauge swatch, check the number of stitches and rows required under the heading "Gauge" at the start of each pattern. The recommended gauge is chosen to give a correct "handle" to the work—too tight, and the work will be firm and heavy; too loose, and it will be floppy and open, and will tend to lose its shape. Stockinette stitch has been used in the following steps for purposes of clarity.

1 Using the correct yarn and needle size for your project, cast on a few more stitches than the number quoted to suit the stitch repeat stated in the gauge instructions. Knit the number of rows required plus about 2in (5cm)—this enables you to measure within the cast-on and top edge. Bind off the stitches and block your knitting (see page 128). Lay the knitting, with right side uppermost, on a flat surface and calculate the number of stitches by inserting a pin centrally on the fabric, a few stitches in from the left-hand edge.

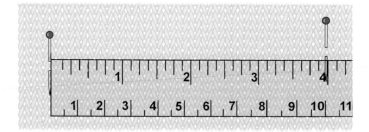

2 Place the end of a tape measure in line with the pin, measure across 4in (10cm), and insert another pin. Remove the tape measure and count the number of stitches (including any half stitches). This is the number of stitches to 4in (10cm).

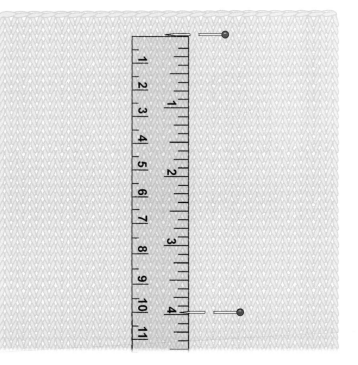

3 To calculate the number of rows, measure 4in (10cm) vertically on a straight line in the center of the fabric and insert two pins exactly 4in (10cm) apart. Remove the tape measure and count the number of rows between the pins. If your gauge matches the recommended gauge exactly, you are ready to start your project. If not, you will need to adjust your gauge (see opposite).

adjusting your gauge

If your knitting has too many stitches or rows to 4in (10cm), your work is too tight and you need to work on larger needles; too few stitches or rows to 4in (10cm) means your work is too loose and you need to work on smaller needles. Change your needle size accordingly and work another gauge swatch. Block the knitting and measure the gauge as before. Repeat this process until your gauge is exactly right. Remember that a small difference over 4in (10cm) can add up to a big difference over the complete project.

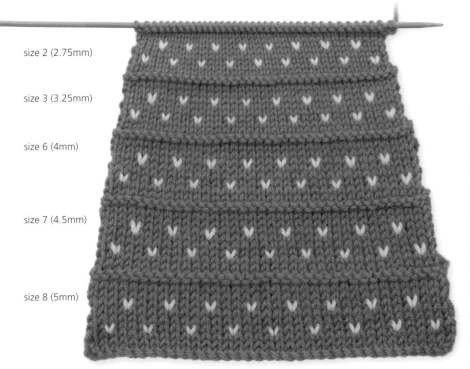

size 2 (2.75mm)

size 3 (3.25mm)

size 6 (4mm)

size 7 (4.5mm)

size 8 (5mm)

Size difference
You can alter the gauge of your knitting with just a change in needle size. The knitted sample shows how the fabric is loose when knitted on larger needles, size 8 (5mm); and tighter when knitted on smaller needles, size 2 (2.75mm).

Knitting needle conversion chart

US SIZES	METRIC SIZES (mm)
0	2.0
1	2.25
2	2.75
–	3.0
3	3.25
4	3.5
5	3.75
6	4.0
7	4.5
8	5.0
9	5.5
10	6.0
10½	6.5
–	7.0
–	7.5
11	8.0
13	9.0
15	10.0
17	12.0
19	16.0
35	19.0
50	25.0

lesson 11

circular knitting

Traditional Fair Isle garments are usually knitted in the round on a set of four double-pointed needles or a circular needle. The right side of the knitting is always facing, which allows you to see your pattern and watch its progression—this method of knitting also creates a seam-free garment.

four double-pointed needles

Four double-pointed needles are used when there are too few stitches to fit on a circular needle—when knitting gloves and mitts, for example. The needles should be long enough to hold a third of the total number of stitches.

Tip

A marker can be placed on the first needle to indicate the beginning of the round.

1 Cast on the required number of stitches using ordinary knitting needles. With the first of the double-pointed needles, slip a third of the stitches purlwise off the ordinary needle. Slip the next third of the stitches onto the second double-pointed needle.

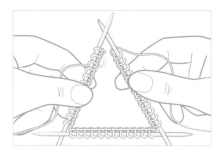

2 Slip the final third of the stitches onto the third double-pointed needle, then push all of the stitches toward the center of each needle. Arrange the needles in a triangle, with the leading top of each needle overlapping the next needle.

Tip

Keep the needles close together and work the first and last stitches on each needle quite tightly to avoid gaps and loose stitches.

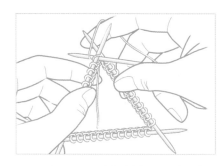

3 To knit a round, hold the needles with the working yarn at the top and on the outside of the triangle. Using the fourth double-pointed needle, knit the stitches on the first needle. Push the stitches toward the center of the needle.

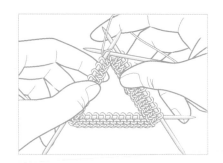

4 With the empty needle, knit the stitches on the second needle, then use the empty needle to knit the stitches on the third needle. Continue in this way, using the empty needle to knit the stitches on the next needle.

circular needles

Circular needles are perfect for knitting larger projects in the round. They are available in different lengths (see page 14), choose the length most suited to your project.

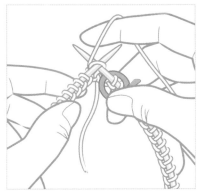

1 Cast on the number of stitches required. Mark the beginning of the round by placing a ring marker or a loop of thread in a contrasting color onto the tip of the right-hand needle. Bring the needle ends together, making sure that the stitches are not twisted around the needle.

2 With the yarn outside the circle, knit the stitches from the left-hand needle onto the right-hand needle, pushing the stitches to be worked along the left-hand needle, so all the stitches slip around the cord.

3 When you reach the marker you will have completed one round. Slip the marker from the left-hand needle onto the right-hand needle and work the next round. The right side of the knitting is always facing you.

hiding the jog

At the beginning of each round you may see a step in the color pattern— this is called a jog. If your color pattern is only one row high, you can usually adjust this when you weave in the yarn ends, but if you are working two or more rounds with the color, this step can be avoided by slipping the first stitch of the second round purlwise without knitting it. The slipped stitch pulls up the ends of the round to the same height, so concealing the step.

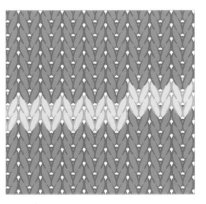

When color knitting in the round, a noticeable step in the fabric occurs.

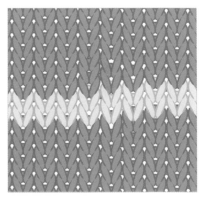

Slipping the first stitch of the round minimizes the step.

lesson 12

holding the yarns

In traditional Fair Isle knitting, no more than two colors are worked in a row. There are several ways of holding the yarn—five methods are shown below. Practice each method to find which suits you best.

one yarn in each hand

The color in your left hand will appear slightly more dominant than the color in your right hand.

Hold the background color in your right hand and the pattern color in your left hand. Knit the stitches in the background color by moving it into place with your right index finger, and the pattern color by picking it up with the tip of the right needle, and pulling it through the stitch and off the needle.

Tip

The yarn at the left is the more dominant color. When you hold the yarns, one color is carried above the other. It is important to keep the yarns in the same position throughout.

both yarns in one hand

There are two ways you can hold the yarns in one hand—both yarns over your index finger, or one yarn over your index finger and the other over your middle finger. The color held over your middle finger will appear more dominant.

Both yarns in one hand—over index finger

With the pattern color to the left of the background color, wrap both yarns around your index finger from front to back. Knit the stitches by selecting the yarn required with the tip of the needle and pulling the yarn through the stitch and off the needle.

Both yarns in one hand—over index and middle fingers

Hold the yarns with the background color over your index finger and the pattern color over your middle finger. Knit the stitches using your index finger to take the background color around the needle, and turn your hand slightly to take the pattern color around with your middle finger.

Tip

If you prefer to hold both yarns over your index finger, there are special yarn guides to help separate the two yarns— see page 15 for more details.

lesson
13

stranding

When knitting Fair Isle patterns, the color not in use is carried across the wrong side of the knitting until it is required again. This forms loose strands on the wrong side of the knitting—these are called floats.

on a knit row

Colors are stranded one above the other between color blocks, producing floats on the wrong side. For an even appearance, it is important that the floats lie consistently either below or above the other. When stranding the yarns, carry them loosely. If the floats are too tight, the fabric will distort the pattern.

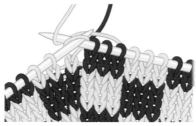

1 Spread out the stitches in the first color just worked on the right-hand needle, to ensure that the float will be the correct length behind the stitches. Knit with the second color, stranding it below the first color.

2 Spread out the stitches worked in the second color, then knit the next group of stitches with the first color, stranding it above the second color.

Tip

Stitches knitted from the color carried below will appear slightly larger than those knitted in the color carried above, and will dominate the color pattern. Therefore, it is important to keep the colors in the same position throughout your Fair Isle pattern.

on a purl row

On the wrong side of the fabric you can see the floats, making it easy to see whether you are stranding the yarn too loosely or too tightly.

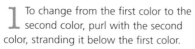

1 To change from the first color to the second color, purl with the second color, stranding it below the first color.

2 Purl the next group of stitches with the first color, stranding it above the second color.

lesson 14 | weaving

When a color passes over a large group of stitches, it should be woven in at the back of one or more of these stitches to prevent long, loose floats on the wrong side of the fabric.

weaving with both hands

Weaving in makes a denser, less flexible fabric than simple stranding, but avoids having long floats that can so easily be caught.

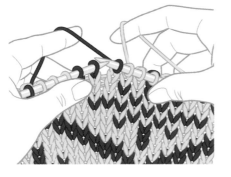

1 To weave the background color, work to the point where the yarn needs to be woven.

2 Take your index finger to the left, laying the background color across the pattern color.

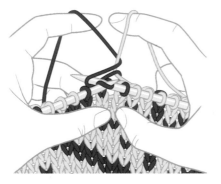

3 Take the right-hand needle over the background color and insert it into the next stitch on the left-hand needle. Pick up the pattern color with the tip of the right-hand needle and pull it through the stitch and off the needle. Take the background color back to its original position and continue knitting.

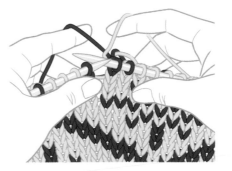

4 To weave the pattern color, work to the point where the yarn needs to be woven. Insert the right-hand needle into the next stitch and under the pattern color, and then knit the stitch with the background color, so weaving the pattern color.

weaving with the right hand

The yarn to be woven is draped across the working yarn and caught up when the stitch is knitted.

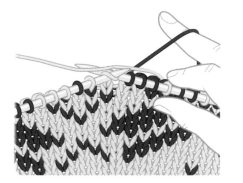 

1 To weave the background color, work to the point where the yarn needs to be woven. Take the background color across the pattern color, then knit the pattern color. Move the background color back to the original position and continue knitting.

2 To weave the pattern color, work to the point where the yarn needs to be woven. Lay the pattern color across the background color and knit the stitch with the background color. Move the pattern color back to the original position and continue knitting.

weaving with the left hand

Both yarns are held in the left hand and the needle is used to pick up the working yarn, catching in the yarn to be woven.

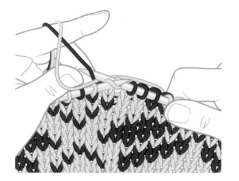 

1 To weave the background color, work to the point where the yarn needs to be woven. Insert the right-hand needle into the next stitch; use your thumb to bring the background color forward. Bring the right-hand needle tip behind the pattern color, from right to left, pick up the pattern color and pull it through the stitch and off the needle. Release the yarn from your thumb and continue knitting.

2 To weave the pattern color, work to the point where the pattern color needs to be woven. Insert the right-hand needle into the next stitch and, with the tip of the needle, reach under the pattern color and catch the background color from right to left, then pull it through the stitch and off the needle. Continue knitting.

Tip

Try to avoid weaving dark colors across large areas of a light color because the woven float may show through on the right side of the fabric. Always stagger where you catch the floats to avoid a vertical line appearing on the right side.

lesson 15 | charts

The stitch patterns in this book have been both written and charted. A chart gives a clear visual impression of how the color sequences will appear, and indicates the number of stitches and rows in a pattern repeat.

reading charts

Charts are read from the bottom to the top following the direction of the knitting. When you reach the top of the chart, begin again at row 1 unless stated otherwise.

Each square on the chart represents one stitch; each horizontal line of squares represents one row. The numbers on each side of the chart indicate the row number, the right- and wrong-side rows, and the pattern repeat.

The corrugated ribbing patterns on pages 40–43 have purl stitches worked on right-side rows and knit stitches worked on wrong-side rows. These stitches are shown by a symbol in the colored square. The symbols represent an instruction and have been designed to resemble the appearance of the knitting.

rows and repeats

The numbers on the right of the chart indicate the right-side rows, and the numbers on the left the wrong-side rows. Check the position of row 1 before you start so that you know whether this is a right- or wrong-side row. Right-side rows are always read from right to left and wrong-side rows from left to right. Most Fair Isle knitting is worked in stockinette stitch, so every right-side row is knit and every wrong-side row is purl.

When knitting in the round, every round is worked in knit stitch, and the right side of the work is always facing. Therefore, the chart should be read from right to left on every round.

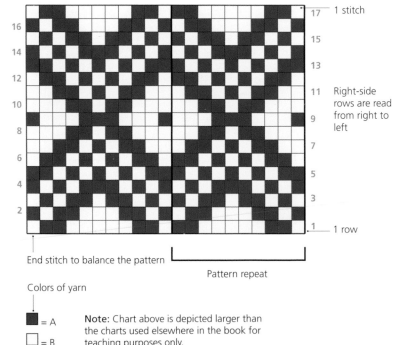

Wrong-side rows are read from left to right

Right-side rows are read from right to left

1 stitch

1 row

End stitch to balance the pattern

Pattern repeat

Colors of yarn

■ = A
□ = B

Note: Chart above is depicted larger than the charts used elsewhere in the book for teaching purposes only.

Tip

When knitting Fair Isle patterns, the yarn not in use is stranded or woven across the wrong side of the knitting—see pages 31–33 for more details.

stitch repeats

The number of stitches required to work a pattern repeat are indicated at the bottom of the chart; here you will also find the end stitches required to balance the pattern when working in rows. When working in rounds, the end stitches are omitted.

If you want to work more than one band of patterning on your design, you need to make sure that the pattern repeats divide into the number of stitches required for your project. If you are working bands of bold patterning, they will need to sit comfortably together so that they are pleasing to the eye—staggered patterns can make a fabric look messy.

You can adjust the pattern repeat to make it fit by adjusting a section of the pattern. Experiment reducing and enlarging motifs on graph paper, then chart them together to make sure that you are happy with the final pattern.

6 rows repeated three times

4-st repeat

Two Fair Isle bands and a seeding pattern have been used to create this beautiful fabric.

27 rows worked once

12-st repeat

5 rows repeated three times with 4 rounds worked in A between repeats

10-st repeat

Yarn colors

= A   = B

Fair Isle patterns

From corrugated ribbing and seeding and Fair Isle bands and patterns, this section showcases knitted samples in an array of wonderful colors. Utilize your newfound skills in one of the 11 gorgeous projects featured in this section.

stitch guide

Select from one of the many Fair Isle patterns featured here, turn to the relevant page number, and start knitting.

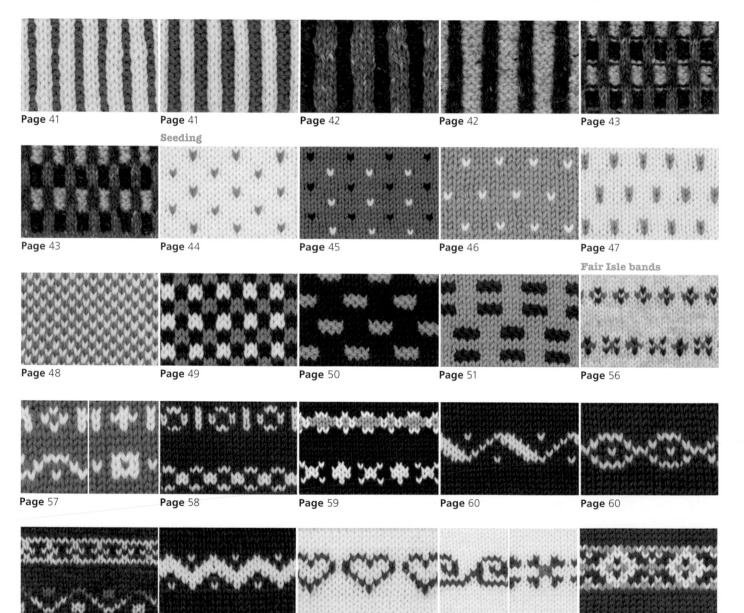

Corrugated ribbing

Page 40   Page 40

Page 41   Page 41   Page 42   Page 42   Page 43

Seeding

Page 43   Page 44   Page 45   Page 46   Page 47

Fair Isle bands

Page 48   Page 49   Page 50   Page 51   Page 56

Page 57   Page 58   Page 59   Page 60   Page 60

Page 61   Page 62   Page 62   Page 63   Page 64

Page 64

Page 65

Page 66

Page 67

Page 68

Page 69

Page 70

Page 71

Page 72

Page 73

Page 74

Page 75

Page 76

Page 77

Page 78

Fair Isle patterns

Page 79

Page 90

Page 91

Page 92

Page 93

Page 94

Page 95

Page 96

Page 97

Page 98

Page 100

Page 101

Page 102

Page 104

Page 105

Page 106

Page 108

Page 110

Page 112

Page 114

lesson 16 | corrugated ribbing

Corrugated ribbing is often used to introduce the colors of the main Fair Isle pattern into the lower edges, cuffs, neck bands, and even button bands of garments. The ribbing is worked as normal in alternating knit and purl stitches, but two or more colors are used to create beautiful and decorative ribbed edges.

Although it looks complex, corrugated ribbing is easy to work. The knit stitches are worked in one color and the purl stitches in another. You can keep the colors the same for a vertical striped effect or reverse them every few rows to create checked patterns. The yarns are stranded at the back of the work in the usual way.

As with all stranded knitting, the resulting ribbed fabric has less give than plain ribbing, and a corrugated ribbing does not gather in as closely. If a tight ribbing is required, the corrugated ribbing can be worked on needles two sizes smaller than those used for the main body of the work.

1 x 1 ribbing

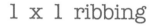

Worked on a multiple of 2 stitches plus 1.

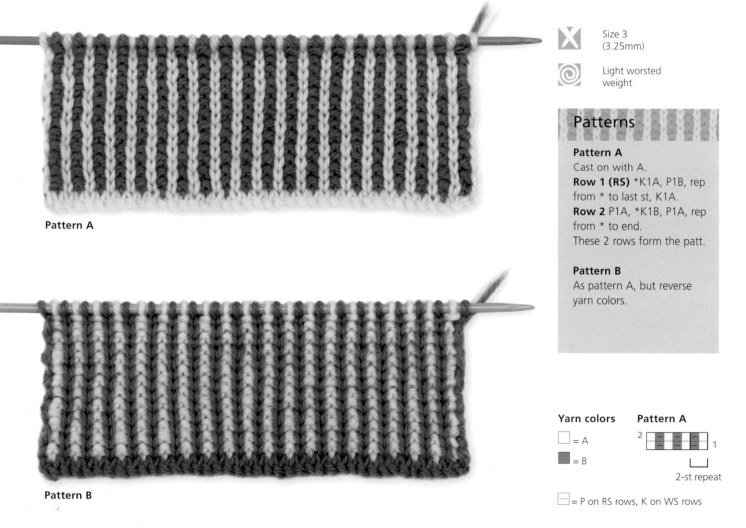

Pattern A

Pattern B

X Size 3 (3.25mm)

◎ Light worsted weight

Patterns

Pattern A
Cast on with A.
Row 1 (RS) *K1A, P1B, rep from * to last st, K1A.
Row 2 P1A, *K1B, P1A, rep from * to end.
These 2 rows form the patt.

Pattern B
As pattern A, but reverse yarn colors.

Yarn colors
☐ = A
■ = B

Pattern A
2 ▭▭▭▭▭ 1
2-st repeat

▭ = P on RS rows, K on WS rows

2 x 1 ribbing

Worked on a multiple of 3 stitches plus 2.

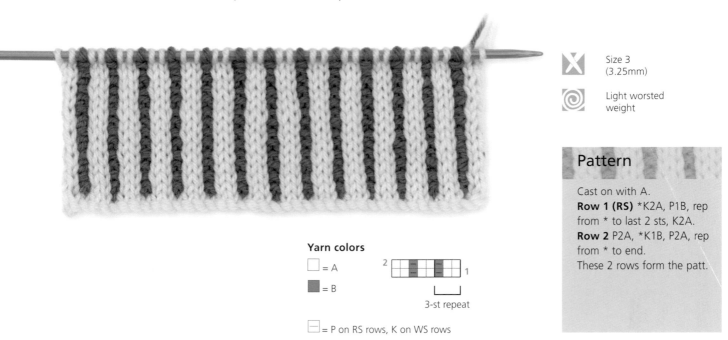

Size 3
(3.25mm)

Light worsted
weight

Yarn colors

☐ = A

■ = B

2 ▢▢▢▢▢▢ 1

3-st repeat

⊟ = P on RS rows, K on WS rows

Pattern

Cast on with A.
Row 1 (RS) *K2A, P1B, rep
from * to last 2 sts, K2A.
Row 2 P2A, *K1B, P2A, rep
from * to end.
These 2 rows form the patt.

2 x 2 ribbing

Worked on a multiple of 4 stitches plus 2.

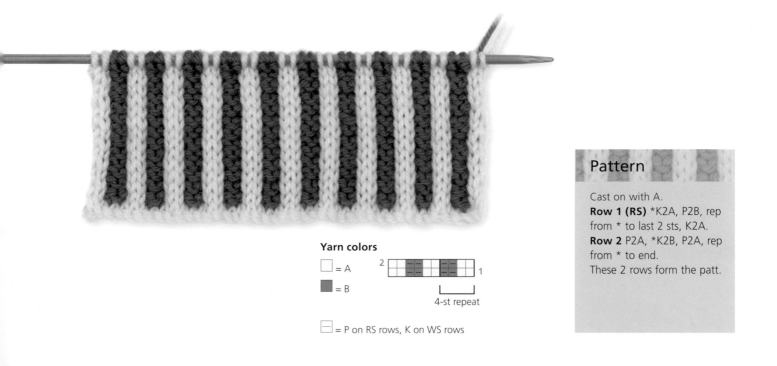

Yarn colors

☐ = A

■ = B

2 ▢▢▢▢▢▢▢ 1

4-st repeat

⊟ = P on RS rows, K on WS rows

Pattern

Cast on with A.
Row 1 (RS) *K2A, P2B, rep
from * to last 2 sts, K2A.
Row 2 P2A, *K2B, P2A, rep
from * to end.
These 2 rows form the patt.

3 x 2 ribbing

Worked on a multiple of 5 stitches plus 3.

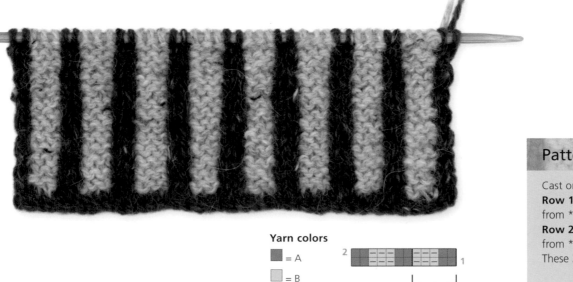

Yarn colors

■ = A
■ = B

□ = P on RS rows, K on WS rows

2 ┃ ┃ 1

5-st repeat

| | Size 3 (3.25mm) |
| | Light worsted weight |

Pattern

Cast on with A.
Row 1 (RS) *K3A, P2B, rep from * to last 3 sts, K3A.
Row 2 P3A, *K2B, P3A, rep from * to end.
These 2 rows form the patt.

2 x 3 ribbing

Worked on a multiple of 5 stitches plus 2.

Yarn colors

■ = A
□ = B

□ = P on RS rows, K on WS rows

2 ┃ ┃ 1

5-st repeat

Pattern

Cast on with A.
Row 1 (RS) *K2A, P3B, rep from * to last 2 sts, K2A.
Row 2 P2A, *K3B, P2A, rep from * to end.
These 2 rows form the patt.

2 x 2 ribbing—with bi-color change

Worked on a multiple of 4 stitches plus 2.

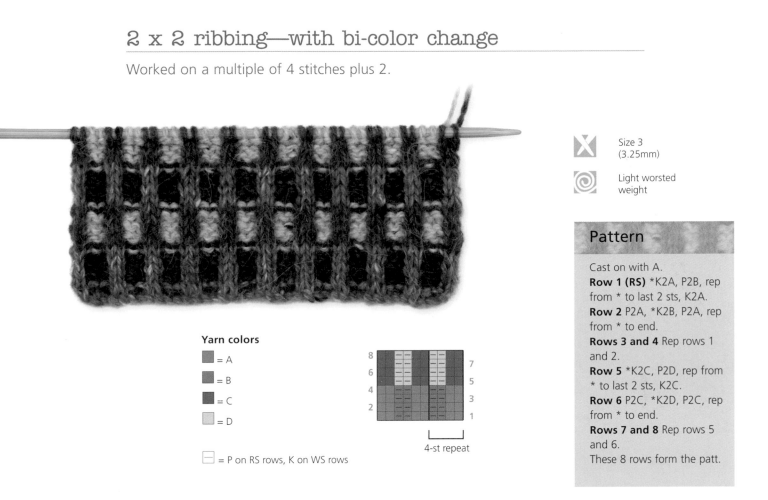

Yarn colors

- ■ = A
- ■ = B
- ■ = C
- ▨ = D

▭ = P on RS rows, K on WS rows

4-st repeat

Pattern

Cast on with A.
Row 1 (RS) *K2A, P2B, rep from * to last 2 sts, K2A.
Row 2 P2A, *K2B, P2A, rep from * to end.
Rows 3 and 4 Rep rows 1 and 2.
Row 5 *K2C, P2D, rep from * to last 2 sts, K2C.
Row 6 P2C, *K2D, P2C, rep from * to end.
Rows 7 and 8 Rep rows 5 and 6.
These 8 rows form the patt.

Size 3
(3.25mm)

Light worsted
weight

2 x 2 ribbing—with smooth color change

For a smooth color change, work as above but knit every stitch in the row where the new color is introduced.

lesson 17

seeding

Seeding is the name given to small patterns that are used to cover areas where a large intricate design is not required. Instead, the background color is punctuated with single stitches or small designs in contrasting colors to introduce a change of pace into the design.

seeding pattern 1

This sample shows five pattern repeats. Worked on a multiple of 6 stitches plus 1.

Areas of seeding are an important design element in a piece of Fair Isle knitting. Used between Fair Isle bands, these small all-over patterns serve an important design purpose by highlighting the area of intricate motifs. They can also be used to create simple patterning over bigger areas of a design or for a complete design, and are often used in places where

shaping would disrupt large patterns. Seeding patterns are created by single stitches or small groups of contrasting stitches repeated at regular intervals. Yarns are stranded or woven across the back of the work in the normal way, depending on the spacing between seeded stitches.

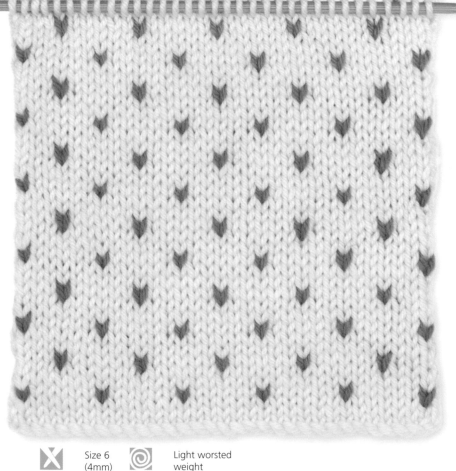

Pattern

Row 1 (RS) With A, K to end.
Row 2 With A, P to end.
Row 3 *K1B, 5A, rep from * to last st, 1B.
Row 4 With A, P to end.
Row 5 With A, K to end.
Row 6 P1A, *2A, 1B, 3A, rep from * to end.
These 6 rows form the patt.

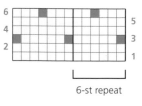

6-st repeat

Yarn colors

☐ = A

■ = B

Size 6 (4mm)

Light worsted weight

variation

Worked in three colors on a
multiple of 6 stitches plus 1.

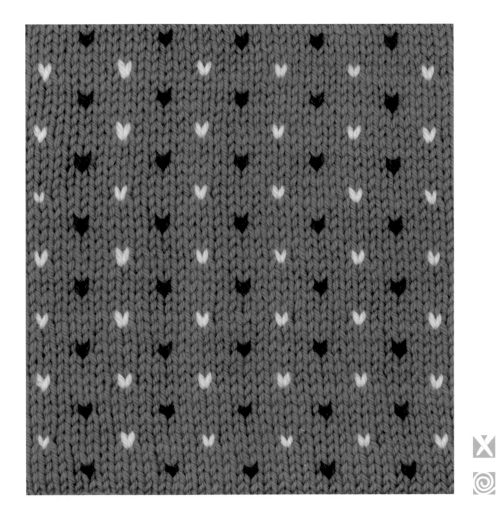

Size 6
(4mm)

Light worsted
weight

Pattern

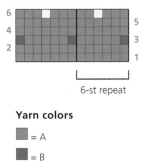

Row 1 (RS) With A, K to end.
Row 2 With A, P to end.
Row 3 *K1B, 5A, rep from * to last st, 1B.
Row 4 With A, P to end.
Row 5 With A, K to end.
Row 6 P1A, *2A, 1C, 3A, rep from * to end.
These 6 rows form the patt.

6-st repeat

Yarn colors

■ = A

■ = B

□ = C

seeding pattern 2

This sample shows seven
pattern repeats. Worked on a
multiple of 4 stitches plus 1.

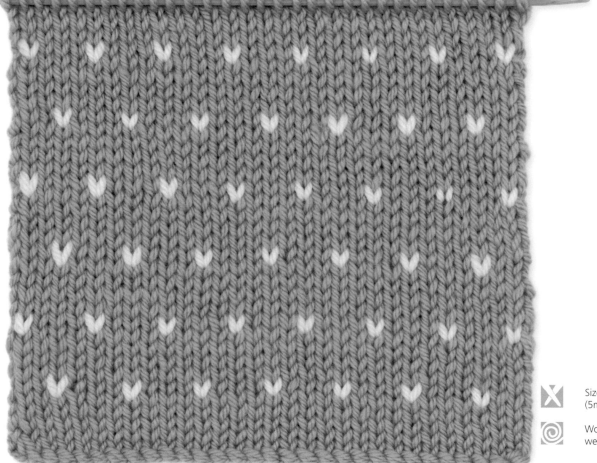

Size 8
(5mm)

Worsted
weight

Pattern

Row 1 (RS) With A, K to end.
Row 2 With A, P to end.
Rows 3 and 4 Rep rows 1 and 2.
Row 5 *K2A, 1B, 1A, rep from * to last st, 1A.
Row 6 With A, P to end.
Rows 7 and 8 Rep rows 1 and 2.
Row 9 Rep row 1.
Row 10 P1B, *3A, 1B, rep from * to end.
These 10 rows form the patt.

4-st repeat

Yarn colors

◻ = A
◻ = B

variation

Worked on a multiple
of 4 stitches plus 1.

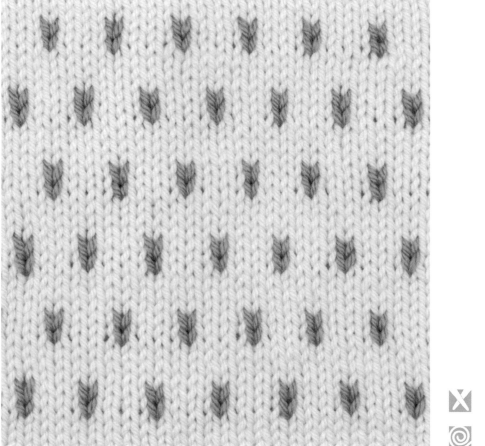

X Size 8
(5mm)

◎ Worsted
weight

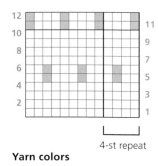

Yarn colors

☐ = A

▨ = B

4-st repeat

Pattern

Row 1 (RS) With A, K to end.
Row 2 With A, P to end.
Rows 3 and 4 Rep rows 1 and 2.
Row 5 *K2A, 1B, 1A, rep from * to last st, 1A.
Row 6 P1A, *1A, 1B, 2A, rep from * to end.
Rows 7 to 10 Rep rows 1 and 2 twice.
Row 11 *K1B, 3A, rep from * to last st, 1B.
Row 12 P1B, *3A, 1B, rep from * to end.
These 12 rows form the patt.

seeding pattern 3

This sample shows 17 pattern repeats. Worked on a multiple of 2 stitches plus 1.

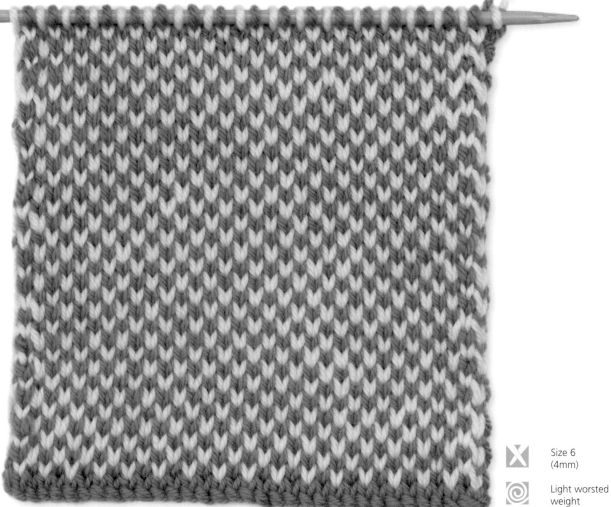

X Size 6 (4mm)

◎ Light worsted weight

2-st repeat

Yarn colors

■ = A

□ = B

Pattern

Row 1 (RS) *K1A, 1B, rep from * to last st, 1A.
Row 2 P1B, *1A, 1B, rep from * to end.
These 2 rows form the patt.

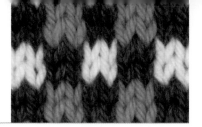

variation

Worked on a multiple
of 4 stitches plus 2.

 Size 6
(4mm)

 Light worsted
weight

Pattern

Row 1 (RS) *K2A, 2B, rep from * to last 2 sts, 2A.
Row 2 P2A, *2B, 2A, rep from to end.
Row 3 *K2C, 2A, rep from * to last 2 sts, 2C.
Row 4 P2C, *2A, 2C, rep from * to end.
These 4 rows form the patt.

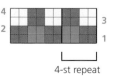

4-st repeat

Yarn colors

■ = A

■ = B

□ = C

seeding pattern 4

This sample shows five pattern repeats. Worked on a multiple of 6 stitches plus 3.

Size 8 (5mm)

Worsted weight

Pattern

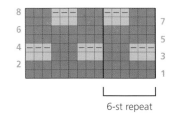

Row 1 (RS) With A, K to end.
Row 2 With A, P to end.
Row 3 *K3B, 3A, rep from * to last 3 sts, 3B.
Row 4 K3B, *P3A, K3B, rep from * to end.
Rows 5 and 6 Rep rows 1 and 2.
Row 7 *K3A, 3B, rep from * to last 3 sts, 3A.
Row 8 P3A, *K3B, P3A, rep from * to end.
These 8 rows form the patt.

6-st repeat

Yarn colors

■ = A

■ = B   ⊟ = K on WS rows

variation

Worked on a multiple
of 6 stitches plus 3.

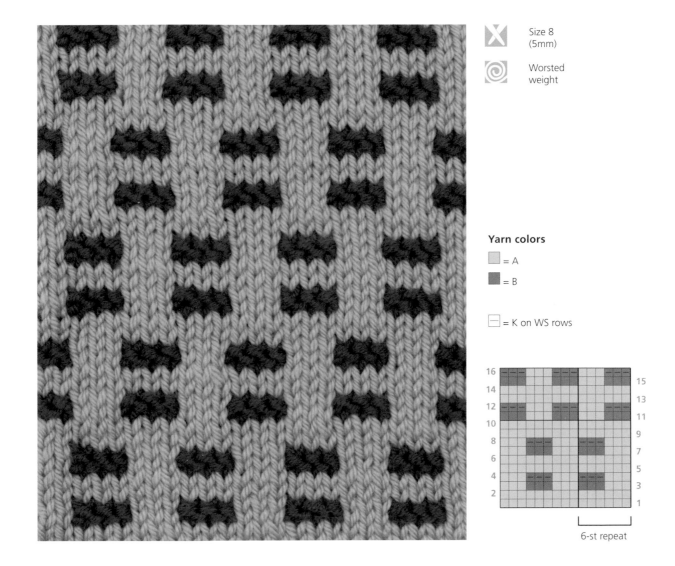

X Size 8
   (5mm)

◎ Worsted
   weight

Yarn colors

▢ = A

▨ = B

▭ = K on WS rows

6-st repeat

Pattern

Row 1 (RS) With A, K to end.
Row 2 With A, P to end.
Row 3 *K3A, 3B, rep from * to last 3 sts,
3A.
Row 4 P3A, *K3B, P3A, rep from * to end.

Rows 5 to 8 Rep rows 1 to 4.
Rows 9 and 10 Rep rows 1 and 2.
Row 11 *K3B, 3A, rep from * to last 3 sts,
3B.
Row 12 K3B, *P3A, K3B, rep from * to end.

Rows 13 and 14 Rep rows 1 and 2.
Rows 15 and 16 Rep rows 11 and 12.
These 16 rows form the patt.

project 1: child's cardigan

This pretty cardigan is knitted in a simple color pattern of stripes and spots and bordered with a cute bell design. Trim the top of each bell with a glossy bead for added interest.

YOU WILL NEED
- 150[200]g light worsted weight yarn in main color (A)
- 100[150]g light worsted weight yarn in contrast color (B)
- 50g light worsted weight yarn in contrast color (C)
- 50g light worsted weight yarn in contrast color (D)
- Size 5 (3.75mm) and size 6 (4mm) knitting needles
- 5 buttons
- 28[32] beads

SIZE
To fit chest 18–20[20–22]in (46–51[51–56]cm)
Actual measurement 21[23½]in (53[60]cm)
Length 9¾[12]in (24.5[30]cm)
Sleeve seam 8¾[9½]in (22[24]cm)

GAUGE
22 sts and 28 rows to 4in (10cm) over seeding patt

Brackets
Figures in square brackets [ ] refer to larger size; where there is only one set of figures, this applies to both sizes.

TO FINISH
Block knitting to size, forming border into "bells." Join sleeve seams, leaving ½in (1cm) open at top of sleeve. Sew sleeves to armholes, sewing ½in (1cm) at top of sleeves to bind-off group at armholes. Press seams. Sew on the buttons. Sew a bead to the top of each "bell."

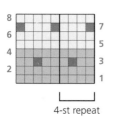

8
6
4
2
7
5
3
1

4-st repeat

Yarn colors
☐ = A
☐ = B
■ = C
■ = D

Pattern

BACK AND FRONTS (worked in one piece to armholes)
Using size 5 (3.75mm) needles and A, cast on 308[352] sts.
Work border patt as follows:
Row 1 (WS) K2, P7, *K4, P7, rep from * to last 2 sts, K2.
Row 2 P2, K7, *P4, K7, rep from * to last 2 sts, P2.
Row 3 Rep row 1.
Row 4 P2, ssk, K3, K2 tog, *P4, ssk, K3, K2 tog, rep from * to last 2 sts, P2.
Row 5 K2, P5, *K4, P5, rep from * to last 2 sts, K2.
Row 6 P2, ssk, K1, K2 tog, *P4, ssk, K1, K2 tog, rep from * to last 2 sts, P2.
Row 7 K2, P3, *K4, P3, rep from * to last 2 sts, K2.
Row 8 P2, sl 2, K1, p2sso, *P4, sl 2, K1, p2sso, rep from * to last 2 sts, P2.
Row 9 K2, P1, *K4, P1, rep from * to last 2 sts, K2.
Join on B.
Next row With B, K4, *K2 tog, K3, rep from * to last st, K1. 113[129] sts.
Change to size 6 (4mm) needles.
Joining on and cutting off colors as required and reading odd numbered (RS) rows from right to left and even numbered (WS) rows from left to right, cont in seeding patt from chart, working in stripes of 4 rows A and 4 rows B until work measures 5½[6¾]in (14[17]cm) from beg, ending with a WS row.
Divide for armholes
Next row Patt 26[30] and leave these sts on a holder for right front, bind off 5 sts, patt until there are 51[59] sts on

right needle and leave these sts on a holder for back, bind off 5 sts, patt to end.
Work on last 26[30] sts for left front as follows:
Dec 1 st at end of next row, then cont on rem 25[29] sts until armhole measures 2¾[3]in (7[8]cm), ending at front edge.
Shape neck
Keeping patt correct, bind off 4[5] sts at beg of next row, then dec 1 st at neck edge on every row until 14[16] sts rem.
Work 2[5] rows.
Bind off.
With WS of work facing, join yarn to back sts on holder.
Dec 1 st at each end of next row, then cont on rem 49[57] sts until back measures same as left front to shoulder.
Bind off.
Mark 14th[16th] st from each end to denote shoulders.
With WS of work facing, join yarn to right front sts on holder.
Dec 1 st at beg of next row, then work on rem 25[29] sts as given for left front.

SLEEVES (alike)
Using size 5 (3.75mm) needles and A, cast on 29[37] sts.
K 3 rows.
Join on B.
With B, K 2 rows.
Change to size 6 (4mm) needles.
Joining on and cutting off colors as required, work 4 rows in seeding patt as for back and fronts.

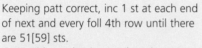

Keeping patt correct, inc 1 st at each end of next and every foll 4th row until there are 51[59] sts.
Cont without shaping until work measures 9[10]in (23[25]cm) from beg. Bind off.

BUTTONHOLE BAND
With RS of work facing, join on A and using size 5 (3.75mm) needles, K up 9 sts along edge of border, then K up 36[44] sts evenly along right front edge to neck. 45[53] sts.
K 1 row.
Buttonhole row (RS) K9, yfd, K2 tog, *K6[8], yfd, K2 tog, rep from * to last 2 sts, K2.
K 2 rows. Bind off knitwise.

BUTTON BAND
With RS of work facing, join on A and using size 5 (3.75mm) needles, K up 36[44] sts evenly along left front edge to border, and 9 sts along border. 45[53] sts.
K 4 rows. Bind off knitwise.

COLLAR
Join shoulder seams. With RS of work facing, join on A and using size 5 (3.75mm) needles, K up 57[67] sts evenly around neck edge.
K 5 rows.
Change to size 6 (4mm) needles and cont in g st until collar measures 2in (5cm), ending with RS facing. Bind off knitwise.

project 2: child's hoodie

This sleeveless top is worked in a crisp cotton yarn for a smart, chic look. It has two front pockets, button fastening at the neck, and a hood worked in the contrast color.

YOU WILL NEED
- 200[250:300]g light worsted weight yarn in main color (A)
- 100[100:150]g light worsted weight yarn in contrast color (B)
- Size 3 (3.25mm) and size 6 (4mm) knitting needles
- Size 3 (3.25mm) circular knitting needle
- 2 buttons

SIZE
To fit chest 20[22:24]in (51[56:61]cm)
Length 10½[12:13]in (27[30:33]cm)

GAUGE
21 sts and 28 rows to 4in (10cm) over seeding patt

Brackets
Figures in square brackets [ ] refer to larger sizes; where there is only one set of figures, this applies to all sizes.

TO FINISH
Block knitting to size. Join side and armband seams. Sew on hood. Sew down ends of front bands and pocket bands. Press seams. Sew on the buttons.

Chart 1

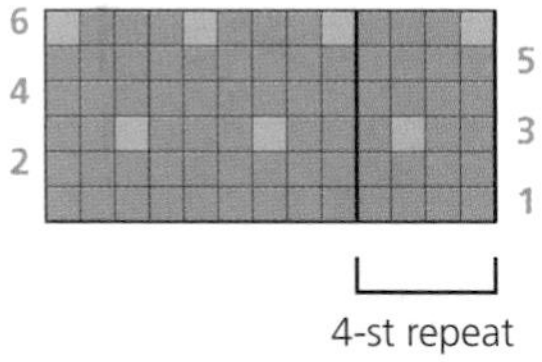

6
4
2

5
3
1

4-st repeat

Chart 2

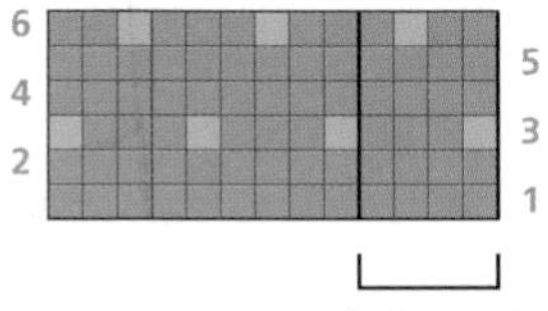

6
4
2

5
3
1

4-st repeat

Yarn colors
■ = A
■ = B

Pattern

BACK
Using size 3 (3.25mm) straight needles and A, cast on 62[66:70] sts.
Rib row 1 (RS) K2, *P2, K2, rep from * to end.
Rib row 2 P2, *K2, P2, rep from * to end.
Rep these 2 rows 3 times more, but dec 1 st at center of last row. 61[65:69] sts.
Change to size 6 (4mm) needles.
Join on B and reading odd numbered (RS) rows from right to left and even numbered (WS) rows from left to right, cont in seeding patt from chart 1 until work measures 5½[6¼:7]in (14[16:18]cm) from beg, ending with a RS row.
Shape armholes
Bind off 4 sts at beg of next 2 rows. 53[57:61] sts.
Cont without shaping until armholes measure 5[5½:6]in (13[14:15]cm), ending with a WS row.
Bind off.
Mark 13th[14th:15th] st from each end to denote shoulders.

POCKET LININGS (make 2)
Using size 6 (4mm) needles and A, cast on 17 sts.
Beg with a K row, work 17 rows st st, so ending with a K row. Cut off yarn and leave sts on a holder.

FRONT
Work as given for back, but work from chart 2 until work measures 3½in (9cm) from beg, ending with a RS row.

Pocket row (WS) Patt 9[10:11], slip next 17 sts onto a holder and in their place patt the sts of one pocket lining, patt 9[11:13], slip next 17 sts onto a holder and in their place patt the sts of the second pocket lining, patt to end.
Cont as given for back to completion of armhole shaping. 53[57:61] sts.
Cont without shaping until armholes measure 2[2½:2¾]in (5[6:7]cm), ending with a WS row.
Divide for opening
Patt 24[26:28], turn and leave rem sts on a spare needle.
Work on first set of sts until front measures same as back, ending with a WS row.
Next row Bind off 13[14:15], patt to end.
Leave rem 11[12:13] sts on a holder for hood.
With RS of work facing, join yarn to sts on spare needle, bind off 5, patt to end. 24[26:28] sts.
Cont on these sts until front measures same as back, ending with a WS row.
Next row Patt 11[12:13] and slip these sts onto a holder for hood, bind off rem 13[14:15] sts.

HOOD
Join shoulder seams.
With RS of work facing, join on B and using size 6 (4mm) needles, K sts from right side of front, cast on 35[37:39] sts, then K across sts from left side of front. 57[61:65] sts.

Beg row 2, work in seeding patt from chart 1, reading A for B and B for A throughout, until hood measures 8¼[8¾:9]in (21[22:23]cm), ending with a WS row. Bind off.

FRONT AND HOOD EDGING
Join top hood seam.
With RS of work facing, join on A and using size 3 (3.25mm) circular needle, K up 130[138:146] sts up right front opening, around hood edge, and down left front opening.
Working backward and forward in rows, beg rib row 2, work 3 rows in rib as given for back.
Buttonhole row (RS) Rib 4, with yarn at front, K2 tog, rib 6, with yarn at front, K2 tog, rib to end.
Rib 3 more rows. Bind off in rib.

ARMBANDS (alike)
With RS of work facing, join on A and using size 3 (3.25mm) needles K up 62[66:70] sts evenly along armhole edge.
Beg rib row 2, work 5 rows in rib as given for back. Bind off in rib.

POCKET BANDS (alike)
With WS of work facing, join on A and using size 3 (3.25mm) needles, P sts from holder, but inc 1 st at the center. 18 sts.
Beg rib row 1, work 4 rows in rib as given for back. Bind off in rib.

lesson 18

Fair Isle bands

Fair Isle bands are horizontal patterns created over a set number of rows. A single band can be used alone as a border in a plain knitted background. Alternatively, several bands of different widths can be combined to build up a layered pattern that can be used once or repeated over the fabric.

Border patterns are generally between 8 and 15 rows deep. A band that is less than 8 rows deep is known as a "peerie," or small pattern. Peeries are often interspersed between larger bands. They are also used alone as pretty decorations for small items such as

baby clothes where a wide border would be overpowering and inappropriate. Worked against backgrounds that contrast with the main background color, peeries also create extra design impact and add to the intricate appearance of a Fair Isle design.

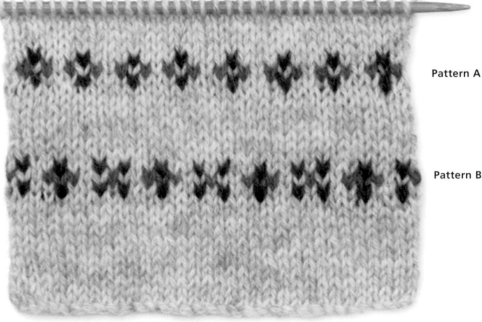

Pattern A

Pattern B

3-row peeries

Pattern A is worked on a multiple of 4 stitches plus 1.

Pattern B is worked on a multiple of 8 stitches plus 1.

Pattern A

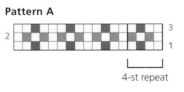

4-st repeat

Pattern B

8-st repeat

Yarn colors

☐ = A

■ = B

■ = C

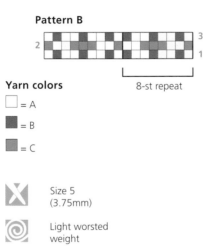

Size 5
(3.75mm)

Light worsted
weight

Patterns

Pattern A
Row 1 (RS) *K2A, 1B, 1A, rep from * to last st, 1A.
Row 2 P1A, *1C, 1A, rep from * to end.
Row 3 Rep row 1.
These 3 rows form the patt.

Pattern B
Row 1 (RS) *K1A, 1B, (2A, 1B) twice, rep from * to last st, 1A.
Row 2 P1C, *2A, 3C, 2A, 1C, rep from * to end.
Row 3 Rep row 1.
These 3 rows form the patt.

variations

Pattern A is worked on a multiple of 8 stitches plus 1.
Pattern B is worked on a multiple of 8 stitches plus 1.
Pattern C is worked on a multiple of 6 stitches plus 1.
Pattern D is worked on a multiple of 6 stitches plus 1.

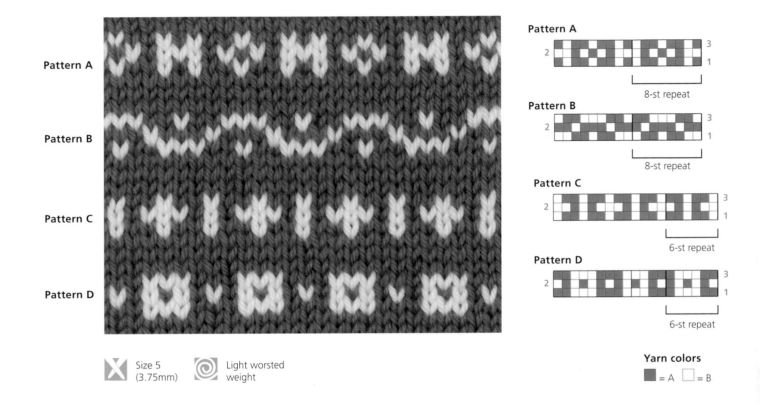

Pattern A

Pattern B

Pattern C

Pattern D

Pattern A

2 ___ 3
1

└─ 8-st repeat ─┘

Pattern B

2 ___ 3
1

└─ 8-st repeat ─┘

Pattern C

2 ___ 3
1

└─ 6-st repeat ─┘

Pattern D

2 ___ 3
1

└─ 6-st repeat ─┘

Size 5
(3.75mm)

Light worsted
weight

Yarn colors

■ = A   □ = B

Patterns

Pattern A
Row 1 (RS) *K1A, 1B, (2A, 1B) twice, rep from * to last st, 1A.
Row 2 P1B, *(1B, 1A) 3 times, 2B, rep from * to end.
Row 3 Rep row 1.
These 3 rows form the patt.

Pattern B
Row 1 (RS) *K2B, (2A, 1B) twice, rep from * to last st, 1B.
Row 2 P1A, *1A, 1B, 3A, 1B, 2A, rep from * to end.

Row 3 *K1B, 2A, 3B, 2A, rep from * to last st, 1B.
These 3 rows form the patt.

Pattern C
Row 1 (RS) *K1B, 2A, rep from * to last st, 1B.
Row 2 P1B, *(1B, 1A) twice, 2B, rep from * to end.
Row 3 Rep row 1.
These 3 rows form the patt.

Pattern D
Row 1 (RS) *K2A, 3B, 1A, rep from * to last st, 1A.
Row 2 P1B, *1A, 1B, rep from * to end.
Row 3 Rep row 1.
These 3 rows form the patt.

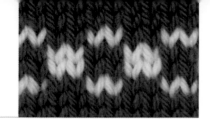

4-row peeries

Pattern A is worked on a multiple of 7 stitches.

Pattern B is worked on a multiple of 4 stitches plus 2.

Pattern A

Pattern B

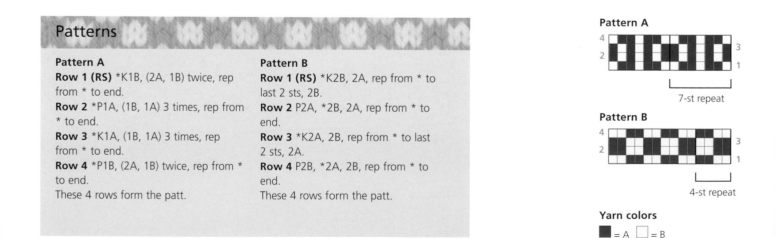

Patterns

Pattern A
Row 1 (RS) *K1B, (2A, 1B) twice, rep from * to end.
Row 2 *P1A, (1B, 1A) 3 times, rep from * to end.
Row 3 *K1A, (1B, 1A) 3 times, rep from * to end.
Row 4 *P1B, (2A, 1B) twice, rep from * to end.
These 4 rows form the patt.

Pattern B
Row 1 (RS) *K2B, 2A, rep from * to last 2 sts, 2B.
Row 2 P2A, *2B, 2A, rep from * to end.
Row 3 *K2A, 2B, rep from * to last 2 sts, 2A.
Row 4 P2B, *2A, 2B, rep from * to end.
These 4 rows form the patt.

Size 6 (4mm)

Light worsted weight

Pattern A
7-st repeat

Pattern B
4-st repeat

Yarn colors
■ = A □ = B

variations

Pattern A is worked on a multiple of 7 stitches.

Pattern B is worked on a multiple of 9 stitches plus 1.

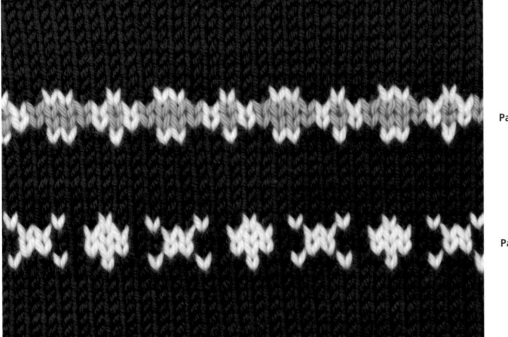

Pattern A

Pattern B

Size 6
(4mm)

Light worsted
weight

Pattern A

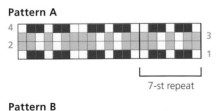

7-st repeat

Pattern B

9-st repeat

Yarn colors

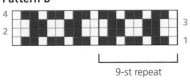 = A □ = B ▨ = C

Patterns

Pattern A
Row 1 (RS) *K1B, (2A, 1B) twice, rep from * to end.
Row 2 *P2C, 1B, 1C, 1B, 2C, rep from * to end.
Row 3 *K2C, 1B, 1C, 1B, 2C, rep from * to end.
Row 4 *P1B, (2A, 1B) twice, rep from * to end.
These 4 rows form the patt.

Pattern B
Row 1 (RS) *K1B, 2A, rep from * to last st, 1B.
Row 2 P1B, *1B, (2A, 2B) twice, rep from * to end.
Row 3 *(K2B, 2A) twice, 1B, rep from * to last st, 1B.
Row 4 P1B, *2A, 1B, rep from * to end.
These 4 rows form the patt.

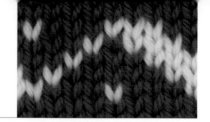

5-row peeries

Pattern A is worked on a multiple of 10 stitches plus 1.

Pattern B is worked on a multiple of 7 stitches.

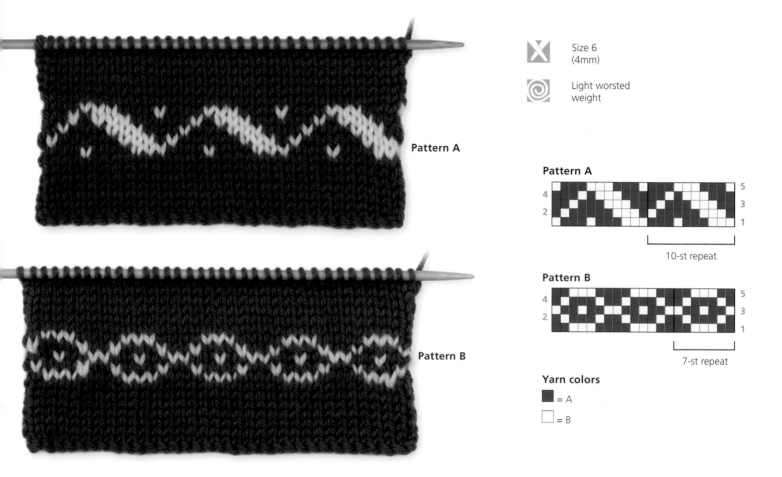

Pattern A

Pattern B

Size 6 (4mm)

Light worsted weight

Pattern A

10-st repeat

Pattern B

7-st repeat

Yarn colors

■ = A

□ = B

Patterns

Pattern A
Row 1 (RS) *K3B, 3A, 1B, 3A, rep from * to last st, 1B.
Row 2 P1A, *1B, 5A, 3B, 1A, rep from * to end.
Row 3 *K2A, 3B, 3A, 1B, 1A, rep from * to last st, 1A.
Row 4 P1A, *2A, 1B, 1A, 3B, 3A, rep from * to end.

Row 5 *K1B, 3A, 3B, 3A, rep from * to last st, 1B.
These 5 rows form the patt.

Pattern B
Row 1 (RS) *K2A, 3B, 2A, rep from * to end.

Row 2 *P1A, 1B, 3A, 1B, 1A, rep from * to end.
Row 3 *K1B, (2A, 1B) twice, rep from * to end.
Row 4 Rep row 2.
Row 5 Rep row 1.
These 5 rows form the patt.

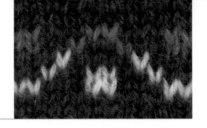

variations

Pattern A is worked on a
multiple of 4 stitches plus 1.

Pattern B is worked on a
multiple of 10 stitches plus 2.

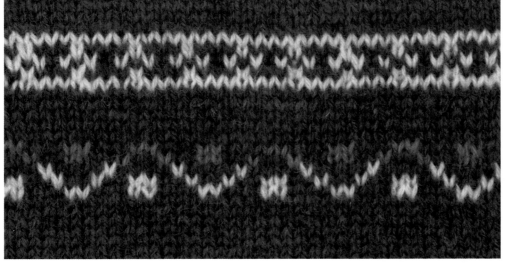

Pattern A

Pattern B

Size 6
(4mm)

Light worsted
weight

Pattern A

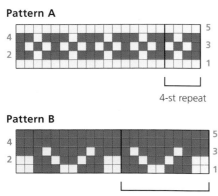

4-st repeat

Pattern B

10-st repeat

Yarn colors

■ = A ☐ = B ■ = C

Patterns

Pattern A
Row 1 (RS) With B, K to end.
Row 2 P1A, *1A, 1B, 2A, rep from * to end.
Row 3 *K1A, 1B, rep from * to last st, 1A.
Row 4 Rep row 2.
Row 5 With B, K to end.
These 5 rows form the patt.

Pattern B
Row 1 (RS) *(K2B, 3A) twice, rep from
* to last 2 sts, 2B.
Row 2 P2B, *2A, (1B, 2A) twice, 2B, rep
from * to end.
Row 3 *K3A, 1B, 4A, 1B, 1A, rep from
* to last 2 sts, 2A.
Row 4 P2A, *1C, 2A, 2C, 2A, 1C, 2A,
rep from * to end.
Row 5 *(K2C, 3A) twice, rep from * to last
2 sts, 2C.
These 5 rows form the patt.

6-row peeries

Pattern A is worked on a
multiple of 6 stitches plus 1.

Pattern B is worked on a
multiple of 8 stitches plus 1.

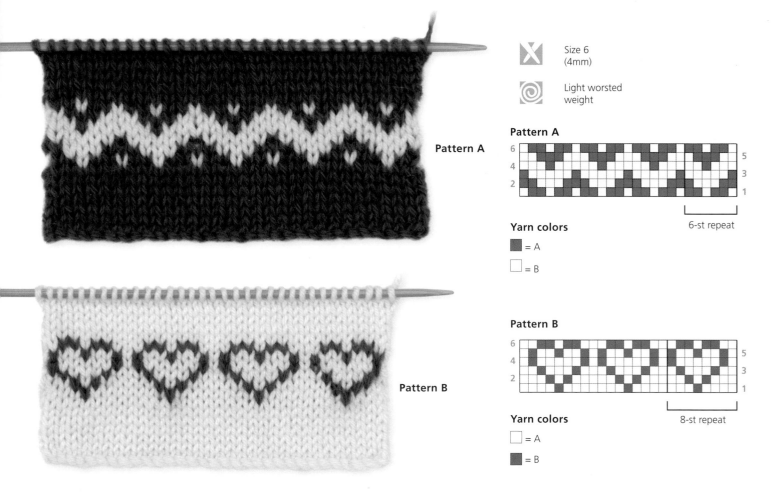

Pattern A

Pattern B

Size 6
(4mm)

Light worsted
weight

Pattern A

6-st repeat

Yarn colors

■ = A

□ = B

Pattern B

8-st repeat

Yarn colors

□ = A

■ = B

Patterns

Pattern A
Row 1 (RS) *K1B, 2A, rep from
* to last st, 1B.
Row 2 P1A, *1A, 3B, 2A, rep from
* to end.
Row 3 *K1A, 5B, rep from * to last st, 1A.
Row 4 P1B, *2B, 1A, 3B, rep from
* to end.
Row 5 *K2B, 3A, 1B, rep from * to
last st, 1B.

Row 6 P1B, *2A, 1B, rep from * to end.
These 6 rows form the patt.

Pattern B
Row 1 (RS) *K4A, 1B, 3A, rep from *
to last st, 1A.
Row 2 P1A, *2A, 1B, 1A, 1B, 3A, rep from
* to end.

Row 3 *K2A, 1B, 3A, 1B, 1A, rep from *
to last st, 1A.
Row 4 P1A, *1B, 5A, 1B, 1A, rep from
* to end.
Row 5 *K1A, 1B, (2A, 1B) twice, rep from
* to last st, 1A.
Row 6 P1A, *(1A, 2B) twice, 2A, rep from
* to end.
These 6 rows form the patt.

variations

Pattern A is worked on a multiple of 8 stitches.

Pattern B is worked on a multiple of 7 stitches plus 1.

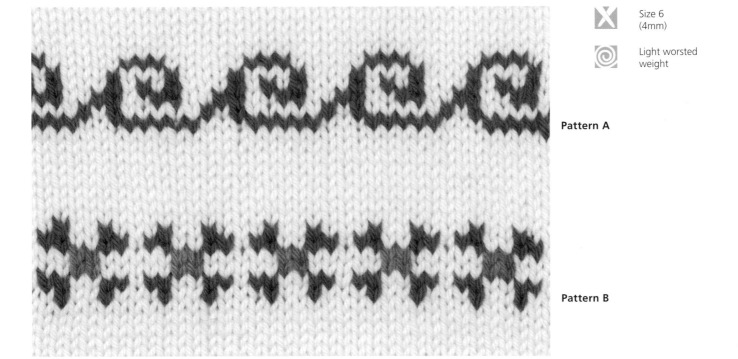

Pattern A

Pattern B

Size 6 (4mm)

Light worsted weight

Pattern A

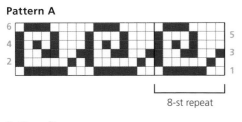

6
4
2
5
3
1

8-st repeat

Pattern B

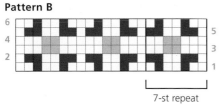

6
4
2
5
3
1

7-st repeat

Yarn colors

□ = A   ■ = B   ▨ = C

Patterns

Pattern A
Row 1 (RS) *K2A, 5B, 1A, rep from * to end.
Row 2 *P1B, 5A, 1B, 1A, rep from * to end.
Row 3 *K1B, 2A, 2B, 2A, 1B, rep from * to end.
Row 4 *P1B, (1A, 1B) twice, 3A, rep from * to end.
Row 5 *K3A, 1B, rep from * to end.
Row 6 *P1A, 3B, 4A, rep from * to end.
These 6 rows form the patt.

Pattern B
Row 1 (RS) *(K2A, 1B) twice, 1A, rep from * to last st, 1A.
Row 2 P1A, *2B, 2A, 2B, 1A, rep from * to end.
Row 3 *K3A, 2C, 2A, rep from * to last st, 1A.
Row 4 P1A, *2A, 2C, 3A, rep from * to end.
Row 5 *K1A, 2B, 2A, 2B, rep from * to last st, 1A.
Row 6 P1A, *1A, (1B, 2A) twice, rep from * to end.
These 6 rows form the patt.

7-row peeries

Pattern A is worked on a multiple of 10 stitches plus 1.

Pattern B is worked on a multiple of 12 stitches plus 1.

Pattern A

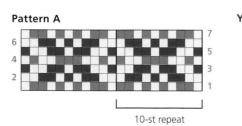

Pattern B

Patterns

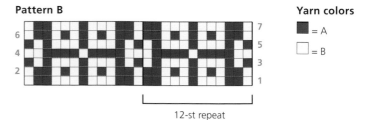

Pattern A
Row 1 (RS) *K1B, 2C, 1B, (1C, 1B) twice, 2C, rep from * to last st, 1B.
Row 2 P1B, *1B, 2A, 1B, 1A, 1B, 2A, 2B, rep from * to end.
Row 3 *K1A, 2B, 2A, 1B, 2A, 2B, rep from * to last st, 1A.
Row 4 P1B, *1C, 2B, 3C, 2B, 1C, 1B, rep from * to end.
Rows 5 to 7 Rep rows 3 to 1 in this order. These 7 rows form the patt.

Pattern B
Row 1 (RS) *K1B, 2A, 3B, 1A, 3B, 2A, rep from * to last st, 1B.
Row 2 P1B, *2A, 1B, (1A, 1B) 3 times, 2A, 1B, rep from * to end.
Row 3 *K1A, 1B, 1A, (3B, 1A) twice, 1B, rep from * to last st, 1A.
Row 4 P1B, *(1B, 4A) twice, 2B, rep from * to end.
Rows 5 to 7 Rep rows 3 to 1 in this order. These 7 rows form the patt.

Size 6 (4mm)

Light worsted weight

Pattern A

6																				7
4																				5
2																				3
																				1

10-st repeat

Yarn colors

■ = A
□ = B
▨ = C

Pattern B

6																				7
4																				5
2																				3
																				1

12-st repeat

Yarn colors

■ = A
□ = B

variations

Pattern A is worked on a multiple of 12 stitches plus 2.

Pattern B is worked on a multiple of 10 stitches plus 1.

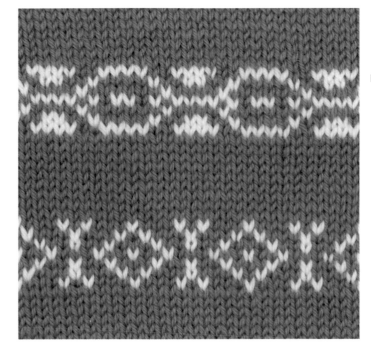

Pattern B

Pattern A

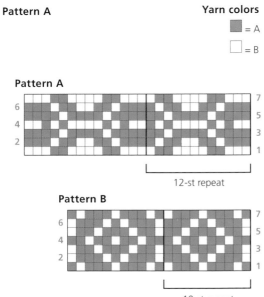

Yarn colors

■ = A

□ = B

Pattern A

12-st repeat

Pattern B

10-st repeat

Size 6
(4mm)

Light worsted weight

Patterns

Pattern A
Row 1 (RS) *K3B, 2A, 4B, 2A, 1B, rep from * to last 2 sts, 2B.
Row 2 P2A, *1A, 1B, 2A, 2B, 2A, 1B, 3A, rep from * to end.
Row 3 *(K4A, 1B) twice, 2A, rep from * to last 2 sts, 2A.
Row 4 P2B, *1A, 1B, 1A, 4B, 1A, 1B, 1A, 2B, rep from * to end.
Rows 5 to 7 Rep rows 3 to 1 in this order.
These 7 rows form the patt.

Pattern B
Row 1 (RS) *K1A, 1B, (3A, 1B) twice, rep from * to last st, 1A.
Row 2 P1B, *3A, 1B, 1A, 1B, 3A, 1B, rep from * to end.
Row 3 *K1B, 2A, 1B, 3A, 1B, 2A, rep from * to last st, 1B.
Row 4 P1A, *1A, (1B, 2A) 3 times, rep from * to end.
Rows 5 to 7 Rep rows 3 to 1 in this order.
These 7 rows form the patt.

zigzags

This sample shows three pattern repeats and two colorways. Worked on a multiple of 10 stitches plus 1.

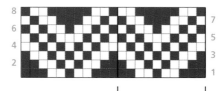

10-st repeat

Size 6 (4mm)

Light worsted weight

Yarn colors

☐ = A

■ = B

Gold has been used for color B on the top band

Pattern

Row 1 (RS) *K3B, 2A, 1B, 2A, 2B, rep from * to last st, 1B.

Row 2 P1B, *1B, 2A, 1B, 1A, 1B, 2A, 2B, rep from * to end.

Row 3 *K1B, 2A, 1B, (1A, 1B) twice, 2A, rep from * to last st, 1B.

Row 4 P1A, *(1A, 1B) 4 times, 2A, rep from * to end.

Row 5 *(K1A, 1B) twice, 3A, 1B, 1A, 1B, rep from * to last st, 1A.

Row 6 P1B, *1A, 1B, (2A, 1B) twice, 1A, 1B, rep from * to end.

Row 7 *K1A, 1B, 2A, 3B, 2A, 1B, rep from * to last st, 1A.

Row 8 P1B, *2A, 5B, 2A, 1B, rep from * to end.

These 8 rows form the patt.

variation

Worked on a multiple of
10 stitches plus 1.

 Size 6
(4mm)

 Light worsted
weight

Pattern

Row 1 (RS) *K1B, 2A, 5B, 2A, rep from * to last st, 1B.

Row 2 P1A, *1B, 2A, 3B, 2A, 1B, 1A, rep from * to end.

Row 3 *K1B, 1A, 1B, (2A, 1B) twice, 1A, rep from * to last st, 1B.

Row 4 P1A, *1B, 1A, 1B, 3A, (1B, 1A) twice, rep from * to end.

Row 5 *K2A, (1B, 1A) 4 times, rep from * to last st, 1A.

Row 6 P1B, *2A, 1B, (1A, 1B) twice, 2A, 1B, rep from * to end.

Row 7 *K2B, 2A, 1B, 1A, 1B, 2A, 1B, rep from * to last st, 1B.

Row 8 P1B, *2B, 2A, 1B, 2A, 3B, rep from * to end.

Row 9 *K1C, 3B, 3C, 3B, rep from * to last st, 1C.

Rows 10 to 17 Rep rows 8 to 1 in this order.

These 17 rows form the patt.

10-st repeat

Yarn colors

◼ = A

☐ = B

◼ = C

flowers

This sample shows two pattern repeats. Worked on a multiple of 14 stitches plus 1.

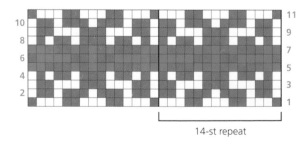

14-st repeat

Yarn colors

■ = A
□ = B
■ = C

   Size 5
(3.75mm)

◎   Light worsted weight

Pattern

Row 1 (RS) *K1A, 3B, (2A, 3B) twice, rep from * to last st, 1A.

Row 2 P1B, *2A, 1B, (3A, 1B) twice, 2A, 1B, rep from * to end.

Row 3 *K1B, 2A, 3B, 3A, 3B, 2A, rep from * to last st, 1B.

Row 4 P1B, *1A, 1B, 2A, 1B, 3A, 1B, 2A, 1B, 1A, 1B, rep from * to end.

Row 5 *K2C, 3A, 1C, (1A, 1C) twice, 3A, 1C, rep from * to last st, 1C.

Row 6 P1A, *4C, 2A, 1C, 2A, 4C, 1A, rep from * to end.

Rows 7 to 11 Rep rows 5 to 1 in this order.

These 11 rows form the patt.

variation

This sample shows the flowers band with two rows of the main color worked at the top and bottom. The band is inserted on a light background fabric.

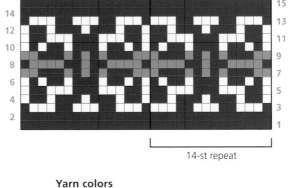

Size 6 (4mm)

Light worsted weight

14-st repeat

Yarn colors

■ = A   □ = B   ▨ = C

Pattern

Row 1 (RS) With A, K to end.
Row 2 With A, P to end.
Row 3 *K1A, 3B, (2A, 3B) twice, rep from * to last st, 1A.
Row 4 P1B, *2A, 1B, (3A, 1B) twice, 2A, 1B, rep from * to end.

Row 5 *K1B, 2A, 3B, 3A, 3B, 2A, rep from * to last st, 1B.
Row 6 P1B, *1A, 1B, 2A, 1B, 3A, 1B, 2A, 1B, 1A, 1B, rep from * to end.
Row 7 *K2C, 3A, 1C, (1A, 1C) twice, 3A, 1C, rep from * to last st, 1C.

Row 8 P1A, *4C, 2A, 1C, 2A, 4C, 1A, rep from * to end.
Rows 9 to 15 Rep rows 7 to 1 in this order. These 15 rows form the patt.

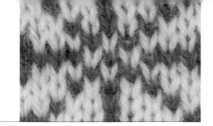

snowflakes

This sample shows two pattern repeats. Worked on a multiple of 14 stitches plus 1.

Size 5
(3.75mm)

Light worsted weight

Pattern

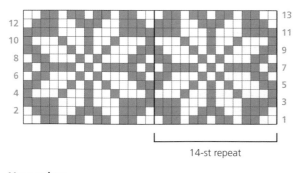

Row 1 (RS) *K2B, 2A, (1B, 2A) 3 times, 1B, rep from * to last st, 1B.
Row 2 P1B, *3A, (2B, 3A) twice, 1B, rep from * to end.
Row 3 *K4A, 3B, 1A, 3B, 3A, rep from * to last st, 1A.
Row 4 P1A, *3B, 1A, (2B, 1A) twice, 3B, 1A, rep from * to end.
Row 5 *K2A, 3B, 1A, (1B, 1A) twice, 3B, 1A, rep from * to last st, 1A.

Row 6 P1B, *2A, 3B, 1A, 1B, 1A, 3B, 2A, !B, rep from * to end.
Row 7 *K1A, 1B, 4A, 1B, 1A, 1B, 4A, 1B, rep from * to last st, 1A.
Rows 8 to 13 Rep rows 6 to 1 in this order.
These 13 rows form the patt.

14-st repeat

Yarn colors

■ = A

□ = B

variation

Worked on a multiple of
14 stitches plus 1.

Size 5
(3.75mm)

Light worsted
weight

Pattern

Row 1 (RS) With B, K to end.
Row 2 P1B, *1B, 1A, 2B, 1A,
3B, (1A, 2B) twice, rep from
* to end.
Row 3 *K1C, 6A, rep from
* to last st, 1C.
Row 4 P1A, *1C, 2A, 1C, 5A,
1C, 2A, 1C, 1A, rep from *
to end.
Row 5 *K1C, 3A, (2C, 3A)
twice, rep from * to last
st, 1C.
Row 6 P1A, *3A, 3B, 1A,
3B, 4A, rep from * to end.
Row 7 *K1A, 3B, 1A, (2B,
1A) twice, 3B, rep from *

to last st, 1A.
Row 8 P1A, *1A, 3B, 1A, (1B,
1A) twice, 3B, 2A, rep from *
to end.
Row 9 *K1B, 2A, 3B, 1A, 1B,
1A, 3B, 2A, rep from * to last
st, 1B.
Row 10 P1A, *1C, 4A, 1C,
1A, 1C, 4A, 1C, 1A, rep from
* to end.
Rows 11 to 19 Rep rows 9
to 1 in this order.
These 19 rows form the patt.

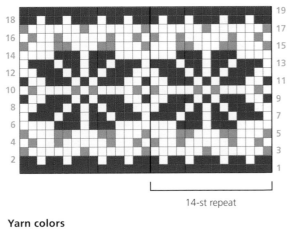

14-st repeat

Yarn colors

☐ = A
■ = B
■ = C

geometric

This sample shows one pattern repeat. Worked on a multiple of 30 stitches plus 1.

X   Size 5 (3.75mm)

◎   Light worsted weight

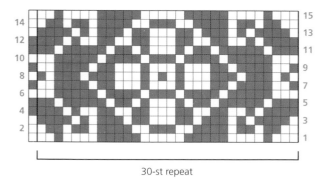

14
12
10
8
6
4
2

15
13
11
9
7
5
3
1

30-st repeat

Yarn colors

■ = A

☐ = B

Pattern

Row 1 (RS) *K3B, 1A, 4B, 5A, 5B, 5A, 4B, 1A, 2B, rep from * to last st, 1B.

Row 2 P1B, *1B, (2A, 1B) twice, 4A, 2B, 3A, 2B, 4A, (1B, 2A) twice, 2B, rep from * to end.

Row 3 *K1B, 4A, 1B, 1A, 1B, 3A, 1B, 2A, 3B, 2A, 1B, 3A, 1B, 1A, 1B, 4A, rep from * to last st, 1B.

Row 4 P1A, *3A, 1B, 1A, (2B, 2A) twice, 3B, (2A, 2B) twice, 1A, 1B, 4A, rep from * to end.

Row 5 *K3A, 1B, 5A, 1B, 2A, 1B, 1A, 3B, 1A, 1B, 2A, 1B, 5A, 1B, 2A, rep from * to last st, 1A.

Row 6 P1B, *2B, 5A, 1B, 4A, 1B, 3A, 1B, 4A, 1B, 5A, 3B, rep from * to end.

Row 7 *K1A, 2B, 4A, 1B, 2A, 3B, (1A, 3B) twice, 2A, 1B, 4A, 2B, rep from * to last st, 1A.

Row 8 P1B, *1A, (1B, 3A) twice, 3B, 1A, (1B, 1A) twice, 3B, (3A, 1B) twice, 1A, 1B, rep from * to end.

Rows 9 to 15 Rep rows 7 to 1 in this order. These 15 rows form the patt.

variation

This sample shows the pattern worked in five colors. The band is inserted on a medium background fabric.

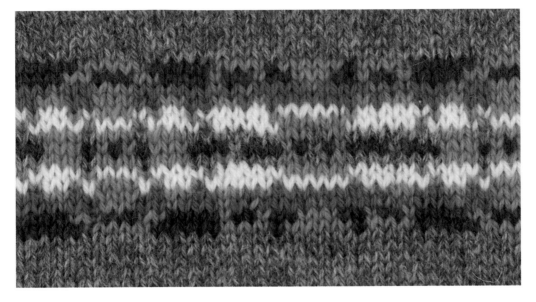

 Size 5 (3.75mm)

Light worsted weight

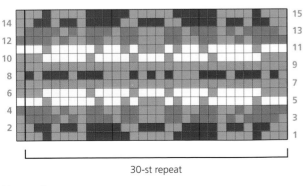

30-st repeat

Yarn colors

■ = A   ■ = C   ■ = E
■ = B   □ = D

Pattern

Row 1 (RS) *K3B, 1A, 4B, 5A, 5B, 5A, 4B, 1A, 2B, rep from * to last st, 1B.

Row 2 P1B, *1B, (2A, 1B) twice, 4A, 2B, 3A, 2B, 4A, (1B, 2A) twice, 2B, rep from * to end.

Row 3 *K1B, 4C, 1B, 1C, 1B, 3C, 1B, 2C, 3B, 2C, 1B, 3C, 1B, 1C, 1B, 4C, rep from * to last st, 1B.

Row 4 P1C, *3C, 1B, 1C, (2B, 2C) twice, 3B, (2C, 2B) twice, 1C, 1B, 4C, rep from * to end.

Row 5 *K3D, 1B, 5D, 1B, 2D, 1B, 1D, 3B, 1D, 1B, 2D, 1B, 5D, 1B, 2D, rep from * to last st, 1D.

Row 6 P1B, *2B, 5D, 1B, 4D, 1B, 3D, 1B, 4D, 1B, 5D, 3B, rep from * to end.

Row 7 *K1E, 2B, 4E, 1B, 2E, 3B, (1E, 3B) twice, 2E, 1B, 4E, 2B, rep from * to last st, 1E.

Row 8 P1B, *1A, (1B, 3A) twice, 3B, 1A, (1B, 1A) twice, 3B, (3A, 1B) twice, 1A, 1B, rep from * to end.

Rows 9 to 15 Rep rows 7 to 1 in this order.

These 15 rows form the patt.

large snowflake

This sample shows one pattern repeat, plus 3 stitches at each end. Worked on a multiple of 24 stitches plus 1.

  Size 5
(3.75mm)

Light worsted weight

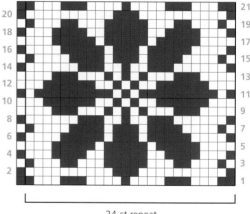

24-st repeat

Yarn colors

☐ = A

■ = B

Pattern

Row 1 (RS) *K2B, 3A, 3B, 4A, 1B, 4A, 3B, 3A, 1B, rep from * to last st, 1B.

Row 2 P1B, *10A, 3B, 10A, 1B, rep from * to end.

Row 3 *K1A, 1B, 3A, 2B, 3A, 5B, 3A, 2B, 3A, 1B, rep from * to last st, 1A.

Row 4 P1B, *3A, 4B, 2A, 5B, 2A, 4B, 3A, 1B, rep from * to end.

Row 5 *K4A, 5B, (1A, 5B) twice, 3A, rep from * to last st, 1A.

Row 6 P1B, *4A, 5B, 1A, 3B, 1A, 5B, 4A, 1B, rep from * to end.

Row 7 *K1A, 1B, 4A, 4B, 1A, 3B, 1A, 4B, 4A, 1B, rep from * to last st, 1A.

Row 8 P1B, *6A, 3B, 2A, 1B, 2A, 3B, 6A, 1B, rep from * to end.

Row 9 *K4A, 3B, 3A, 1B, (1A, 1B) twice, 3A, 3B, 3A, rep from * to last st, 1A.

Row 10 P1A, *2A, 6B, 2A, 1B, 1A, 1B, 2A, 6B, 3A, rep from * to end.

Row 11 *K1B, 1A, 9B, 1A, 1B, 1A, 9B, 1A, rep from * to last st, 1B.

Rows 12 to 21 Rep rows 10 to 1 in this order. These 21 rows form the patt.

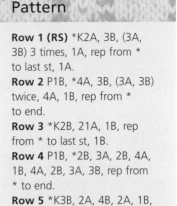

variation

Worked on a multiple of 24 stitches plus 1.

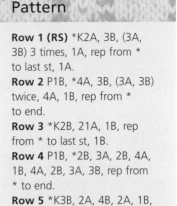

Size 5 (3.75mm)

Light worsted weight

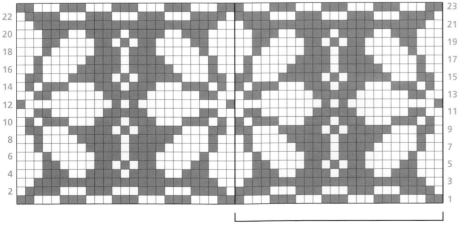

24-st repeat

Yarn colors

■ = A □ = B

Pattern

Row 1 (RS) *K2A, 3B, (3A, 3B) 3 times, 1A, rep from * to last st, 1A.

Row 2 P1B, *4A, 3B, (3A, 3B) twice, 4A, 1B, rep from * to end.

Row 3 *K2B, 21A, 1B, rep from * to last st, 1B.

Row 4 P1B, *2B, 3A, 2B, 4A, 1B, 4A, 2B, 3A, 3B, rep from * to end.

Row 5 *K3B, 2A, 4B, 2A, 1B, 1A, 1B, 2A, 4B, 2A, 2B, rep from * to last st, 1B.

Row 6 P1B, *2B, 1A, 5B, 3A, 1B, 3A, 5B, 1A, 3B, rep from * to end.

Row 7 *K2B, 1A, 5B, 4A, 1B, 4A, 5B, 1A, 1B, rep from * to last st, 1B.

Row 8 P1B, *1B, 1A, 4B, 5A, 1B, 5A, 4B, 1A, 2B, rep from * to end.

Row 9 *K1B, 2A, 3B, 5A, 1B, 1A, 1B, 5A, 3B, 2A, rep from * to last st, 1B.

Row 10 P1B, *1A, 1B, 3A, 3B, 3A, 1B, 3A, 3B, 3A, 1B, 1A, 1B, rep from * to end.

Row 11 *K2B, 2A, 6B, 5A, 6B, 2A, 1B, rep from * to last st, 1B.

Row 12 P1A, *10B, 1A, 1B, 1A, 10B, 1A, rep from * to end.

Rows 13 to 23 Rep rows 11 to 1 in this order. These 23 rows form the patt.

hearts

This sample shows three pattern repeats. Worked on a multiple of 10 stitches plus 1. The band is inserted on a background worked in color B.

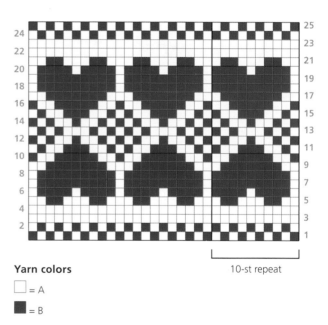

Size 6 (4mm)

Light worsted weight

Yarn colors

☐ = A

■ = B

10-st repeat

Pattern

Row 1 (RS) *K1B, 1A, rep from * to last st, 1B.
Row 2 P1A, *1B, 1A, rep from * to end.
Row 3 With A, K to end.
Row 4 With A, P to end.
Row 5 *K2A, 2B, 3A, 2B, 1A, rep from * to last st, 1A.
Row 6 P1A, *4B, 1A, rep from * to end.

Row 7 *K1A, 9B, rep from * to last st, 1A.
Row 8 P1A, *9B, 1A, rep from * to end.
Row 9 *K2A, 7B, 1A, rep from * to last st, 1A.
Row 10 P1B, *2A, 5B, 2A, 1B, rep from * to end.
Row 11 *K1A, 1B, 2A, 3B, 2A, 1B, rep from * to last st, 1A.

Row 12 P1B, *1A, 1B, (2A, 1B) twice, 1A, 1B, rep from * to end.
Row 13 *(K1A, 1B) twice, 3A, 1B, 1A, 1B, rep from * to last st, 1A.
Rows 14 to 25 Rep rows 12 to 1 in this order.
These 25 rows form the patt.

variation

Worked on a multiple of
10 stitches plus 1.

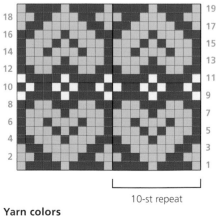

Size 5
(3.75mm)

Light worsted
weight

Yarn colors

■ = A
▨ = B
□ = C

10-st repeat

Pattern

Row 1 (RS) *K1B, 4A, rep from * to last st, 1B.
Row 2 P1B, *1B, 2A, 3B, 2A, 2B, rep from * to end.
Row 3 *K1B, 2A, 5B, 2A, rep from * to last st, 1B.
Row 4 P1A, *(1A, 3B) twice, 2A, rep from * to end.
Row 5 *K1A, 3B, 1A, 1B, 1A, 3B, rep from * to last st, 1A.
Row 6 P1A, *2B, 1A, 3B, 1A, 2B, 1A, rep from * to end.
Row 7 *K1A, 4B, rep from * to last st, 1A.
Row 8 P1A, *1A, 2B, 3A, 2B, 2A, rep from * to end.
Row 9 *K1C, 4A, rep from * to last st, 1C.
Row 10 P1A, *1C, 2A, 1C, 1A, 1C, 2A, 1C, 1A, rep from * to end.
Rows 11 to 19 Work rows 9 to 1 in this order. These 19 rows form the patt.

snowflakes and chevrons

This sample shows three pattern repeats. Worked on a multiple of 12 stitches plus 1. The band is inserted on a background worked in color B.

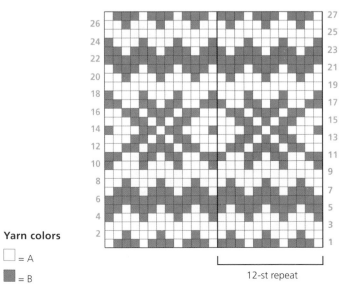

Yarn colors

□ = A

■ = B

26 24 22 20 18 16 14 12 10 8 6 4 2

27 25 23 21 19 17 15 13 11 9 7 5 3 1

12-st repeat

X Size 6 (4mm)

◎ Light worsted weight

Pattern

Row 1 (RS) *K1A, 3B, rep from * to last st, 1A.

Row 2 P2A, 1B, *3A, 1B, rep from * to last 2 sts, 2A.

Row 3 With A, K to end.

Row 4 P1B, *3A, 1B, rep from * to end.

Row 5 K2B, 1A, *3B, 1A, rep from * to last 2 sts, 2B.

Row 6 With B, P to end.

Row 7 Rep row 1.

Row 8 Rep row 2.

Row 9 Rep row 3.

Row 10 P1B, *3A, 1B, rep from * to end.

Row 11 *K2B, 2A, 2B, 1A, 2B, 2A, 1B, rep from * to last st, 1B.

Row 12 P1A, *1A, 2B, 1A, 3B, 1A, 2B, 2A, rep from * to end.

Row 13 *K3A, 2B, 1A, 1B, 1A, 2B, 2A, rep from * to last st, 1A.

Row 14 P1B, *3A, 2B, 1A, 2B, 3A, 1B, rep from * to end.

Rows 15 to 27 Rep rows 13 to 1 in this order.

These 27 rows form the patt.

variations

The snowflakes and chevrons band can be worked in two or more colors. This sample shows four colors.

Size 6 (4mm)

Light worsted weight

Pattern

Row 1 (RS) *K1B, 3A, rep from * to last st, 1B.
Row 2 P2B, 1A, *3B, 1A, rep from * to last 2 sts, 2B.
Row 3 With B, K to end.
Row 4 P1C, *3B, 1C, rep from * to end.
Row 5 K2C, 1B, *3C, 1B, rep from * to last 2 sts, 2C.
Row 6 With C, P to end.
Row 7 *K1A, 3C, rep from * to last st, 1A.
Row 8 K2A, 1C, *3A, 1C, rep from * to last 2 sts, 2A.
Row 9 With A, K to end.
Row 10 P1D, *3A, 1D, rep from * to end.

Row 11 *K2D, 2A, 2D, 1A, 2D, 2A, 1D, rep from * to last st, 1D.
Row 12 P1A, *1A, 2D, 1A, 3D, 1A, 2D, 2A, rep from * to end.
Row 13 *K3A, 2D, 1A, 1D, 1A, 2D, 2A, rep from * to last st, 1A.
Row 14 P1D, *3A, 2D, 1A, 2D, 3A, 1D, rep from * to end.
Rows 15 to 27 Rep rows 13 to 1 in this order.
These 27 rows form the patt.

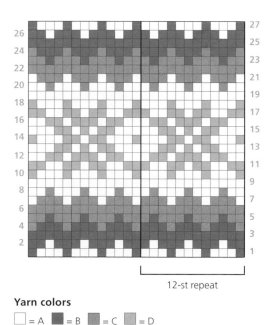

12-st repeat

Yarn colors
☐ = A ▨ = B ▨ = C ▨ = D

project 3: fingerless mitts

A pair of cozy mitts knitted in a soft, fluffy yarn is just the thing to keep your hands warm. The mitts are knitted in seed stitch with a narrow Fair Isle band around the top—so simple!

Pattern

TO MAKE

Using size 5 (3.75mm) needles and A, cast on 39 sts.

Rib row 1 (RS) K1, *P1, K1, rep from * to end.

Rib row 2 P1, *K1, P1, rep from * to end.

Rep these 2 rows for 2in (5cm), ending rib row 2, and inc 1 st at each end of last row. 41 sts.

Change to size 7 (4.5mm) needles.

Now work in sd st as follows:

Sd st row K1, *P1, K1, rep from * to end.

This row forms the patt.

Cont in patt until work measures 4¼in (11cm) from beg, ending with WS facing.

Join on B.

With B, K 1 row and P 1 row.

Joining on and cutting off colors as required and reading odd numbered (RS) rows from right to left and even numbered (WS) rows from left to right, work the 7 rows of Fair Isle patt from chart, so ending with a RS row.

With B, P 1 row and K 1 row.

Cut off B.

Change to size 5 (3.75mm) needles.

With A, P 2 rows.

Bind off knitwise.

Make another mitt in the same way.

YOU WILL NEED
- 50g worsted weight yarn in main color (A)
- 25g worsted weight yarn in contrast color (B)
- 10g worsted weight yarn in contrast color (C)
- Size 5 (3.75mm) and size 7 (4.5mm) knitting needles

SIZE
To fit average size hand
Around palm 7½in (19cm)
Length 6¼in (16cm)

GAUGE
22 sts and 34 rows to 4in (10cm) over sd st

TO FINISH

Weave in the ends. With right sides together, pin the seam on each mitt leaving an opening for the thumb. Carefully try on the mitts and adjust the opening if necessary. Join the seam.

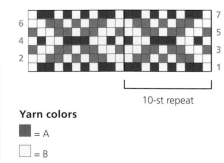

10-st repeat

Yarn colors

■ = A

□ = B

■ = C

project 4: hot water bottle cover

Wrap a hot water bottle in a cozy cover worked in bands of Fair Isle patterning. The two soft shades, cream and mink, are reversed on the seeding pattern for added effect.

YOU WILL NEED
- 50g light worsted weight yarn in main color (A)
- 50g light worsted weight yarn in contrast color (B)
- Size 3 (3.25mm) and size 6 (4mm) circular knitting needles, 16in (40cm) long
- Set of four size 3 (3.25mm) and four size 6 (4mm) double-pointed needles
- 5 buttons
- Thin cardboard
- Pair of compasses and pencil
- Scissors
- Hot water bottle

SIZE
To fit a hot water bottle 8 x 10in (20.5 x 25cm)

GAUGE
26 sts and 30 rows to 4in (10cm) over Fair Isle patt

TO FINISH
Block knitting to size. Weave in the ends, then join bind-off groups at each side of cuff. Sew the buttons to the wrong side of the back to correspond with the buttonholes. Using four 3½yd (3m) lengths of A, make a twisted cord (see page 136). Using ¾in (2cm) circles of cardboard, make 2 pompoms in A (see page 135). Starting at the center front, thread the cord evenly round the base of the cuff. Sew a pompom to each end of the cord. Turn back top of cuff for 1¼in (3cm).

Pattern

TO MAKE
Using size 3 (3.25mm) circular needle and A, cast on 120 sts.
Mark the beg of the round.
Rib round *K1, P1, rep from * to end.
Work the rib round 3 times more.
Buttonhole round Rib 35, yfd, K2 tog, (rib 10, yfd, K2 tog) 4 times, rib 35.
Work 5 more rounds in rib.
Change to size 6 (4mm) circular needle.
K 2 rounds.
Join on B.
**Reading every row from right to left, work the 5 rows of Fair Isle patt from chart 1.
With A, K 4 rounds.**
Rep from ** to ** twice more.
Reading every row from right to left, work the 27 rows of Fair Isle patt from chart 2.
Reading every row from right to left, work the 6 rows of Fair Isle patt from chart 3 twice.
Keeping patt correct, shape top as follows:
Dec round 1 Patt 26, (K2 tog) twice, (ssk) twice, patt 52, (K2 tog) twice, (ssk) twice, patt 26. 112 sts.
Dec round 2 Patt 24, (K2 tog) twice, (ssk) twice, patt 48, (K2 tog) twice, (ssk) twice, patt 24. 104 sts.
Dec round 3 Patt 22, (K2 tog) twice, (ssk) twice, patt 44, (K2 tog) twice, (ssk) twice, patt 22. 96 sts.
Dec round 4 Patt 20, (K2 tog) twice, (ssk) twice, patt 40, (K2 tog) twice, (ssk) twice, patt 20. 88 sts.

Dec round 5 Patt 18, (K2 tog) twice, (ssk) twice, patt 36, (K2 tog) twice, (ssk) twice, patt 18. 80 sts.
Dec round 6 Patt 16, (K2 tog) twice, (ssk) twice, patt 32, (K2 tog) twice, (ssk) twice, patt 16. 72 sts.
Cut off A and cont with B only.
Change to size 6 (4mm) double-pointed needles.
Next round K12, bind off 12, K until there are 24 sts on needle after bind-off group, bind off 12, K to end.
K 1 round on rem 48 sts.
Change to size 3 (3.25mm) double-pointed needles.
Work cuff as follows:
Work the rib round for 2¾in (7cm).
Change to size 6 (4mm) double-pointed needles.
Cont in rib until cuff measures 10cm (4in). Bind off knitwise.

Chart 3

4-st
repeat

Chart 2

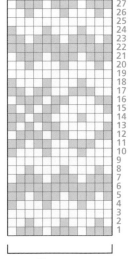

12-st repeat

Chart 1

10-st repeat

Yarn colors

 = A   = B

project 5: beret

A row of striking snowflakes is worked just above the band of corrugated ribbing on this stylish beret.

YOU WILL NEED
• 100g light worsted weight yarn in main color (A)
• 50g light worsted weight yarn in contrast color (B)
• Size 3 (3.25mm) and size 6 (4mm) circular knitting needles, 16in (40cm) long

SIZE
To fit average size head

GAUGE
26 sts to 4in (10cm) over Fair Isle patt
13 rows of Fair Isle patt measure 2in (5cm)

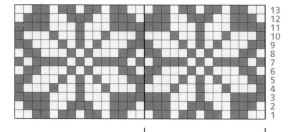

14-st repeat

Yarn colors

 = A

= B

Pattern

TO MAKE
Using size 3 (3.25mm) circular needle and A, cast on 120 sts.
Place a marker on right needle to mark beg of round.
Slipping the marker on every round, join on B and work in rounds of corrugated ribbing as follows:
Round 1 *K2A, P2B, rep from * to end.
Rep this round twice more.
Round 4 *K2B, P2A, rep from * to end.
Rep last round twice more.
Round 7 *K2A, P2B, rep from * to end.
Rep last round twice more.
Inc round With A, (K1, puk) twice, (K2, puk) to last 2 sts, (K1, puk) twice. 182 sts.
Change to size 6 (4mm) circular needle.
With A, K 2 rounds.
Reading every row from right to left, work the 13 rows of Fair Isle patt. Cut off B and cont with A only.
K 4 rounds.
Next round P to form a ridge.
Next round K to end, dec 6 sts evenly. 176 sts.
Next round K to end.
Shape top
Dec round 1 *K2 tog, K18, skpo, rep from * to end. 160 sts.
K 3 rounds.

Dec round 2 *K2 tog, K16, skpo, rep from * to end. 144 sts.
K 3 rounds.
Dec round 3 *K2 tog, K14, skpo, rep from * to end. 128 sts.
K 3 rounds.
Dec round 4 *K2 tog, K12, skpo, rep from * to end. 112 sts.
K 3 rounds.
Dec round 5 *K2 tog, K10, skpo, rep from * to end. 96 sts.
K 3 rounds.
Dec round 6 *K2 tog, K8, skpo, rep from * to end. 80 sts.
K 1 round.
Cont to dec 16 sts on next and every foll alt round, working 2 sts less between each dec until 32 sts rem.
K 1 round.
Next round *K2 tog, skpo, rep from * to end. 16 sts.
K 1 round.
Next round (K2 tog) to end. 8 sts.
Cut off yarn, leaving a 4¾in (12cm) end.
Thread end through rem sts, draw up tightly and secure.
Weave in the ends.

project 6: leg warmers

Pattern—two-needle method

TO MAKE
Using pair of size 3 (3.25mm) needles and A,
cast on 81 sts.
Rib row 1 (RS) K1, *P1, K1, rep from * to end.
Rib row 2 P1, *K1, P1, rep from * to end.
Rep these 2 rows for 2¾in (7cm), ending rib row 1.
Inc row Rib 4, puk, *rib 8, puk, rep from * to last
5 sts, rib 5. 91 sts.
Change to pair of size 6 (4mm) needles.
Joining on and cutting off colors as required and
reading odd numbered (RS) rows from right to left
and even numbered (WS) rows from left to right,
work the 22 rows of Fair Isle patt from chart twice,
then work rows 1 to 5 again, so ending with a
RS row.
Cut off B, C, and D.
Change to pair of size 3 (3.25mm) needles.
Next row With A, P to end.
Now work the 2 rib rows for 3½in (9cm), ending
rib row 2.
Bind off in rib.

Make another leg warmer in the same way.

A Fair Isle band in warm honey
hues is repeated on these comfy
leg warmers. The top and ankle
cuffs are worked in ribbing for
a snug fit.

YOU WILL NEED
• 100g light worsted weight yarn in main color (A)
• 50g light worsted weight yarn in contrast color (B)
• 50g light worsted weight yarn in contrast color (C)
• 50g light worsted weight yarn in contrast color (D)
• Pair each of size 3 (3.25mm) and size 6 (4mm)
  knitting needles or set of four double-pointed
  needles in each of those sizes

SIZE
Length 12in (30cm) with cuff turned back

GAUGE
26 sts and 28 rows to 4in (10cm) over Fair Isle patt

TO FINISH
Weave in the ends.
For two-needle method, join the center back seam.

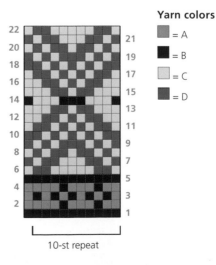

Yarn colors
■ = A
■ = B
□ = C
■ = D

10-st repeat

Pattern—four-needle method

TO MAKE

Using size 3 (3.25mm) double-pointed needles and A, cast 27 sts onto each of first two needles and 26 sts onto third needle. 80 sts. Alternatively, cast on 80 sts using size 3 (3.25mm) ordinary needles and then transfer the sts onto the double-pointed needles, dividing the sts evenly between three of the needles.

Using the fourth double-pointed needle, work in rib as follows:

Rib round *K1, P1, rep from * to end.
Rep this row for 2¾in (7cm).

Inc round Rib 4, puk, *rib 8, puk, rep from * to last 4 sts, rib 4. 90 sts.

Change to size 6 (4mm) double-pointed needles. Joining on and cutting off colors as required and reading all rows from right to left, work the 22 rows of Fair Isle patt from chart twice, then work rows 1 to 5 again.

Cut off B, C, and D.

Change to size 3 (3.25mm) double-pointed needles.

Next round With A, K to end.
Now work the rib round for 3½in (9cm).
Bind off in rib.

Make another leg warmer in the same way.

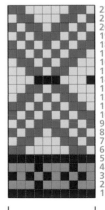

10-st repeat

Yarn colors

= A   ■ = B   = C   ■ = D

project 7: hat and scarf

The hat has a band of heart motifs and is trimmed with a plump tassel. The scarf is worked in seed stitch and finished with two deep pockets.

Pattern—hat

TO MAKE

Using size 7 (4.5mm) needles and A, cast on 101 sts.
Cont in sd st as follows:
Sd st row K1, *P1, K1, rep from * to end.
Rep this row 3 times more.
Change to size 8 (5mm) needles.
Join on B.
Reading odd numbered (RS) rows from right to left and even numbered (WS) rows from left to right, work rows 3 to 23 of Fair Isle patt from chart.
Cut off B and cont with A only.
P 1 row.
Dec row 1 K1, *K2 tog, K8, rep from * to end. 91 sts.
P 1 row.
Dec row 2 K1, *K2 tog, K7, rep from * to end. 81 sts.
P 1 row.
Dec row 3 K1, *K2 tog, K6, rep from * to end. 71 sts.
P 1 row.
Cont to dec in this way, working 1 st less between each dec on next and every alt row until a row has been worked thus: K1, *K2 tog, K1, rep from * to end. 21 sts.
Next row (P2 tog) to last st, P1.
Cut off yarn, leaving a long end. Thread end through rem sts, draw up tightly, and secure.

YOU WILL NEED (for the set)
- 300g worsted weight yarn in main color (A)
- 100g worsted weight yarn in contrast color (B)
- Size 7 (4.5mm) and size 8 (5mm) knitting needles
- Cardboard for tassel

SIZE
Scarf 8 x 67in (20 x 170cm)
Hat to fit average size head

GAUGE
16 sts and 27 rows to 4in (10cm) over sd st

TO FINISH HAT
Block knitting to size. Join center back seam. Using A, make a tassel (see page 134), wrapping yarn around a 3in (8cm) length of cardboard. Sew the tassel to the center top.

TO FINISH SCARF
Block pockets to size. Weave in the ends, then using a long length of A, sew one pocket to each end of the scarf, working blanket stitch over the edge (see designer's tip).

designer's tip

To blanket stitch, working from left to right with the edge you are working on toward you, bring the needle through the knitting from back to front ½in (1cm) to the right and level with the first stitch, bring the point of the needle toward you and over the loop of yarn, and pull through so that the loop lies on the edge of the knitting. Continue in this way.

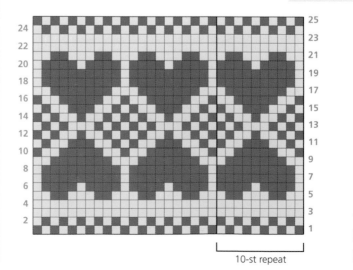

10-st repeat

Yarn colors

= A

= B

Pattern—scarf

TO MAKE
Using size 8 (5mm) needles and A, cast on 31 sts.
Cont in sd st as follows:
Sd st row K1, *P1, K1, rep from * to end.
Rep this row until work measures 67in (170cm) from beg. Bind off.

POCKETS (make 2)
Using size 8 (5mm) needles and B, cast on 31 sts.

Work 3 rows in sd st.
Inc row Patt 3, P1, (pup, P5) twice, pup, P3, pup, (P5, pup) twice, P1, patt 3. 37 sts.
Next row (RS) K1, P1, K1, K to last 3 sts, K1, P1, K1.
Next row K1, P1, K1, P to last 3 sts, K1, P1, K1.
Cont the sd st border in B at each end, work Fair Isle patt over center 31 sts as follows:
Row 1 (RS) Sd st 3, work row 1 of Fair Isle patt to last 3 sts, sd st 3.

Row 2 Sd st 3, work row 2 of Fair Isle patt to last 3 sts, sd st 3.
Cont in patt as set until row 25 has been worked.
Cut off A and cont with B only.
Next row Sd st 3, P to last 3 sts, sd st 3.
Next row Sd st 3, K to last 3 sts, sd st 3.
Dec row Sd st 3, (P2 tog, P4) twice, P2 tog, P3, P2 tog, (P4, P2 tog) twice, sd st 3. 31 sts.
Work 5 rows sd st.
Bind off knitwise.

lesson 19 | Fair Isle patterns

Large Fair Isle patterns can be repeated both vertically and horizontally over the entire knitted surface to create breathtaking fabrics with the endless variety of intricate tonal and pattern variations typical of traditional Fair Isle knitting. Color placement is key to the stunning overall effects created by the technique.

This lesson includes small and large Fair Isle patterns. Large Fair Isle patterns have more than 15 rows and are perfect for bigger items, from sweaters and jackets to throws, pillows, and bags. They often interlock to create intriguing all-over designs.

Large patterns can also work well in combination with border and peerie patterns, while a single pattern repeat can be isolated on the back of mittens or the ends of a scarf for an eye-catching design focus.

small squares

This sample shows nine pattern repeats. Worked on a multiple of 4 stitches plus 1.

Size 5 (3.75mm)

Light worsted weight

Yarn colors

■ = A
■ = B

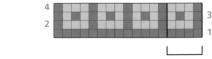

4-st repeat

Pattern

Row 1 (RS) With A, K to end.
Row 2 P1A, *3B, 1A, rep from * to end.
Row 3 *K1A, 1B, rep from * to last st, 1A.
Row 4 Rep row 2.
These 4 rows form the patt.

variation

This sample shows the pattern
worked in three colors.

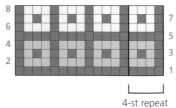

Size 5
(3.75mm)

Light worsted
weight

4-st repeat

Yarn colors

■ = A
■ = B
□ = C

Pattern

Row 1 (RS) With A, K to end.
Row 2 P1A, *3B, 1A, rep from * to end.
Row 3 *K1A, 1B, rep from * to last st, 1A.
Row 4 Rep row 2.
Row 5 With A, K to end.
Row 6 P1A, *3C, 1A, rep from * to end.
Row 7 *K1A, 1C, rep from * to last st, 1A.
Row 8 Rep row 6.
These 8 rows form the patt.

trellis

This sample shows five pattern repeats. Worked on a multiple of 8 stitches plus 1.

Size 6
(4mm)

Light worsted
weight

Pattern

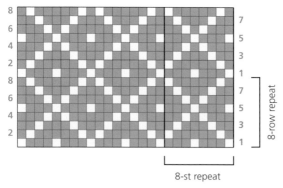

Row 1 (RS) *K1B, 3A, rep from * to last st, 1B.

Row 2 P1A, *1B, 5A, 1B, 1A, rep from * to end.

Row 3 *K2A, 1B, 3A, 1B, 1A, rep from * to last st, 1A.

Row 4 P1A, *2A, 1B, 1A, 1B, 3A, rep from * to end.

Row 5 *K1B, 3A, rep from * to last st, 1B.

Rows 6 to 8 Rep rows 4 to 2 in this order. These 8 rows form the patt.

Yarn colors

■ = A □ = B

variation

A space-dyed yarn has been used as the main color, so introducing more tones into the simple Fair Isle design.

 Size 6
(4mm)

Light worsted
weight

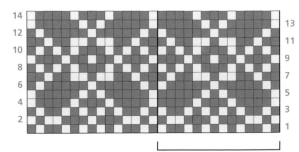

crosses

This sample shows three pattern repeats. Worked on a multiple of 14 stitches plus 1.

Size 6
(4mm)

Light worsted weight

Pattern

Row 1 (RS) *K1A, 1B, 2A, 1B, (1A, 1B) 3 times, 2A, 1B, rep from * to last st, 1A.

Row 2 P1B, *1A, 2B, 3A, 1B, 3A, 2B, 1A, 1B, rep from * to end.

Row 3 Rep row 1.

Row 4 P1B, *4A, 1B, 3A, 1B, 4A, 1B, rep from * to end.

Row 5 *K1B, 5A, 1B, 1A, 1B, 5A, rep from * to last st, 1B.

Row 6 P1A, *1B, (5A, 1B) twice, 1A, rep from * to end.

Row 7 *K2A, 1B, 2A, 2B, 1A, 2B, 2A, 1B, 1A, rep from * to last st, 1A.

Row 8 P1A, *1B, (1A, 1B) twice, 3A, (1B, 1A) 3 times, rep from * to end.

Row 9 *K1B, 3A, 1B, (2A, 1B) twice, 3A, rep from * to last st, 1B.

Rows 10 to 14 Rep rows 8 to 4 in this order.

These 14 rows form the patt.

14-st repeat

Yarn colors

■ = A □ = B

variation

Worked on a multiple of
14 stitches plus 1.

 Size 6
(4mm)

 Light worsted
weight

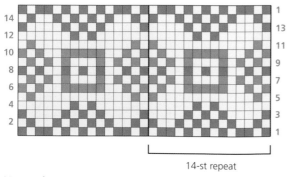

14-st repeat

Yarn colors

☐ = A

■ = B

■ = C

Pattern

Row 1 (RS) *K1B, 1A, 2B, 1A, (1B, 1A) 3 times, 2B, 1A, rep from * to last st, 1B.

Row 2 P1A, *1B, 2A, 1B, (1A, 1B) 3 times, 2A, 1B, 1A, rep from * to end.

Row 3 *K1B, 4A, 1B, (1A, 1B) twice, 4A, rep from * to last st, 1B.

Row 4 P1A, *5A, 1B, 1A, 1B, 6A, rep from * to end.

Row 5 *K1A, 1C, 11A, 1C, rep from * to last st, 1A.

Row 6 P1C, *1A, 1C, 2A, 5C, 2A, 1C, 1A, 1C, rep from * to end.

Row 7 *(K1A, 1C) 3 times, 3A, 1C, (1A, 1C) twice, rep from * to last st, 1A.

Row 8 P1B, *1A, 1B, 2A, 1B, (1A, 1B) twice, 2A, 1B, 1A, 1B, rep from * to end.

Rows 9 to 14 Rep rows 7 to 2 in this order. These 14 rows form the patt.

flowers and diamonds

This sample shows two pattern repeats. Worked on a multiple of 16 stitches plus 1.

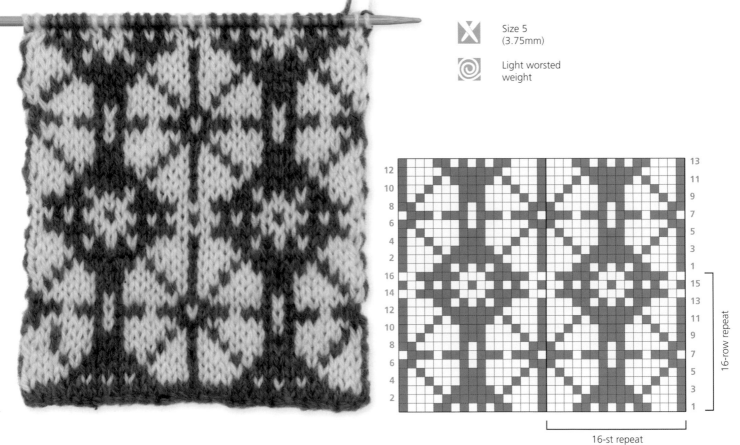

Size 5
(3.75mm)

Light worsted
weight

16-row repeat

16-st repeat

Yarn colors

■ = A

□ = B

Pattern

Row 1 (RS) *K1A, 3B, 2A, 1B, (1A, 1B) twice, 2A, 3B, rep from * to last st, 1A.
Row 2 P1A, *4B, 7A, 4B, 1A, rep from * to end.
Row 3 *K1A, 3B, 1A, 1B, 5A, 1B, 1A, 3B, rep from * to last st, 1A.
Row 4 P1A, *2B, 1A, 3B, 3A, 3B, 1A, 2B,

1A, rep from * to end.
Row 5 *K1A, 1B, 1A, 4B, 3A, 4B, 1A, 1B, rep from * to last st, 1A.
Row 6 P1A, *1A, 5B, 1A, 1B, 1A, 5B, 2A, rep from * to end.
Row 7 *K1B, 3A, rep from * to last st, 1B.
Rows 8 to 13 Rep rows 6 to 1 in this order.

Row 14 P1B, *1B, 5A, 3B, 5A, 2B, rep from * to end.
Row 15 *K1A, 2B, 1A, 1B, 1A, (2B, 1A) twice, 1B, 1A, 2B, rep from * to last st, 1A.
Row 16 Rep row 14.
These 16 rows form the patt.

variation

The flowers and diamonds pattern is shown here in three colors.

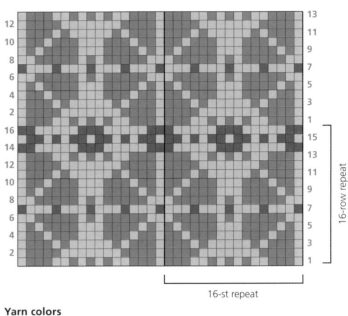

Yarn colors

☐ = A   ■ = B   ■ = C

Size 5
(3.75mm)

Light worsted
weight

Pattern

Row 1 (RS) *K1A, 3B, 2A, 1B, (1A, 1B) twice, 2A, 3B, rep from * to last st, 1A.

Row 2 P1A, *4B, 7A, 4B, 1A, rep from * to end.

Row 3 *K1A, 3B, 1A, 1B, 5A, 1B, 1A, 3B, rep from * to last st, 1A.

Row 4 P1A, *2B, 1A, 3B, 3A, 3B, 1A, 2B, 1A, rep from * to end.

Row 5 *K1A, 1B, 1A, 4B, 3A, 4B, 1A, 1B, rep from * to last st, 1A.

Row 6 P1A, *1A, 5B, 1A, 1B, 1A, 5B, 2A, rep from * to end.

Row 7 *K1C, 3A, rep from * to last st, 1C.

Rows 8 to 13 Rep rows 6 to 1 in this order.

Row 14 P1C, *1C, 5A, 3C, 5A, 2C, rep from * to end.

Row 15 *K1A, 2C, 1A, 1C, 1A, (2C, 1A) twice, 1C, 1A, 2C, rep from * to last st, 1A.

Row 16 Rep row 14.

These 16 rows form the patt.

double diamonds

This sample shows two pattern repeats. Worked on a multiple of 16 stitches plus 1.

 Size 6 (4mm)

 Light worsted weight

Pattern

Row 1 (RS) *K1B, 2A, 1B, 3A, 3B, 3A, 1B, 2A, rep from * to last st, 1B.

Row 2 P1A, *1B, 4A, 2B, 1A, 2B, 4A, 1B, 1A, rep from * to end.

Row 3 *K2A, 1B, 2A, 2B, 3A, 2B, 2A, 1B, 1A, rep from * to last st, 1A.

Row 4 P1B, *3A, 2B, 5A, 2B, 3A, 1B, rep from * to end.

Row 5 *K3A, 2B, 3A, 1B, 3A, 2B, 2A, rep from * to last st, 1A.

Row 6 P1A, *1A, 2B, 4A, 1B, 4A, 2B, 2A, rep from * to end.

Row 7 *K1A, 2B, 3A, 1B, (1A, 1B) twice, 3A, 2B, rep from * to last st, 1A.

Row 8 P1B, *1B, 5A, 1B, 1A, 1B, 5A, 2B, rep from * to end.

Row 9 *K1B, 3A, 3B, 1A, 1B, 1A, 3B, 3A, rep from * to last st, 1B.

Rows 10 to 16 Rep rows 8 to 2 in this order.

These 16 rows form the patt.

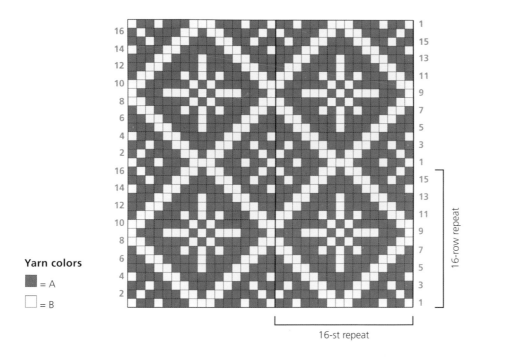

Yarn colors

■ = A
□ = B

variations

The diamond pattern can be worked in two or more colors. These charts show four-color variations.

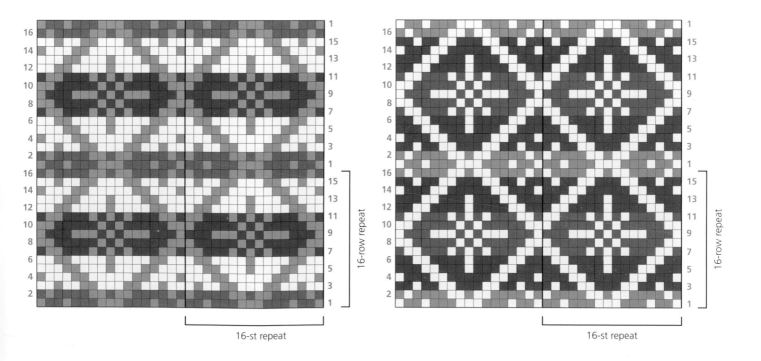

tweed diamonds

This sample shows three pattern repeats. Worked on a multiple of 16 stitches plus 1.

⊠ Size 5 (3.75mm)

◎ Light worsted weight

Pattern

Row 1 (RS) *(K1B, 1A) 3 times, 5B, 1A, (1B, 1A) twice, rep from * to last st, 1B.

Row 2 P1A, *(1B, 1A) twice, (3B, 1A) twice, (1B, 1A) twice, rep from * to end.

Row 3 *(K1B, 1A) twice, 3B, 3A, 3B, 1A, 1B, 1A, rep from * to last st, 1B.

Row 4 P1A, *1B, 1A, 3B, 2A, 1B, 2A, 3B, 1A, 1B, 1A, rep from * to end.

Row 5 *K1B, 1A, 3B, 2A, 1B, 1A, 1B, 2A, 3B, 1A, rep from * to last st, 1B.

Row 6 P1A, *3B, 2A, 1B, 3A, 1B, 2A, 3B, 1A, rep from * to end.

Row 7 *K3B, 2A, 1B, 5A, 1B, 2A, 2B, rep from * to last st, 1B.

Row 8 P1B, *1B, 2A, 1B, 3A, 1B, 3A, 1B, 2A, 2B, rep from * to end.

Row 9 *K1B, 2A, 1B, 3A, 1B, 1A, 1B, 3A, 1B, 2A, rep from * to last st, 1B.

Rows 10 to 16 Rep rows 8 to 2 in this order.
These 16 rows form the patt.

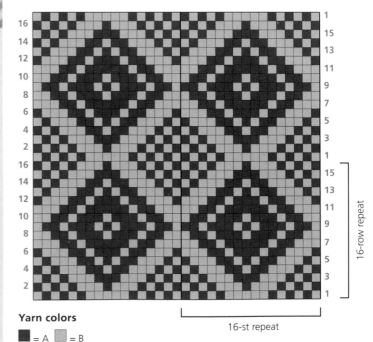

Yarn colors
■ = A ▨ = B

16-row repeat

16-st repeat

variation

Worked on a multiple of
16 stitches plus 1.

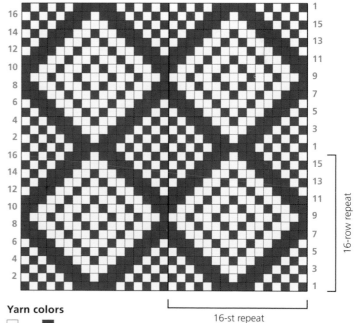

Size 5
(3.75mm)

Light worsted
weight

Pattern

Row 1 (RS) *(K1B, 1A) 3 times, 5B, 1A, (1B, 1A) twice, rep from * to last st, 1B.

Row 2 P1A, *(1B, 1A) twice, (3B, 1A) twice, (1B, 1A) twice, rep from * to end.

Row 3 *(K1B, 1A) twice, 3B, 3A, 3B, 1A, 1B, 1A, rep from * to last st, 1B.

Row 4 P1A, *1B, 1A, 3B, 2A, 1B, 2A, 3B, 1A, 1B, 1A, rep from * to end.

Row 5 *K1B, 1A, 3B, 2A, 1B, 1A, 1B, 2A, 3B, 1A, rep from * to last st, 1B.

Row 6 P1A, *3B, 2A, 1B, 3A, 1B, 2A, 3B, 1A, rep from * to end.

Row 7 *K3B, 2A, (1B, 2A) 3 times, 2B, rep from * to last st, 1B.

Row 8 P1B, *1B, (2A, 1B) twice, 1A, (1B, 2A) twice, 2B, rep from * to end.

Row 9 *K1B, (2A, 1B) twice, 3A, (1B, 2A) twice, rep from * to last st, 1B.

Rows 10 to 16 Rep rows 8 to 2 in this order.
These 16 rows form the patt.

Yarn colors

□ = A ■ = B

16-row repeat

16-st repeat

checked

This sample shows one pattern repeat. Worked on a multiple of 20 stitches plus 10.

X Size 8 (5mm)

◎ Worsted weight

Pattern

Row 1 (RS) *K1B, 8A, 1B, 1A, 8B, 1A, rep from * to last 10 sts, 1B, 8A, 1B.

Row 2 P1A, 1B, 2A, 2B, 2A, 1B, 1A, *1B, 1A, 2B, 2A, 2B, (1A, 1B) twice, 2A, 2B, 2A, 1B, 1A, rep from * to end.

Row 3 *K2A, 1B, 4A, 1B, 2A, 2B, 1A, 4B, 1A, 2B, rep from * to last 10 sts, 2A, 1B, 4A, 1B, 2A.

Row 4 P3A, 1B, 2A, 1B, 3A, *3B, 1A, 2B, 1A, 3B, 3A, 1B, 2A, 1B, 3A, rep from * to end.

Row 5 *K1A, 1B, 2A, 2B, 2A, (1B, 1A) twice, 2B, 2A, 2B, 1A, 1B, rep from * to last 10 sts, 1A, 1B, 2A, 2B, 2A, 1B, 1A.

Row 6 P1A, 1B, 2A, 2B, 2A, 1B, 1A, *1B, 1A, 2B, 2A, 2B, (1A, 1B) twice, 2A, 2B, 2A, 1B, 1A, rep from * to end.

Row 7 *K3A, 1B, 2A, 1B, 3A, 3B, 1A, 2B, 1A, 3B, rep from * to last 10 sts, 3A, 1B, 2A, 1B, 3A.

Row 8 P2A, 1B, 4A, 1B, 2A, *2B, 1A, 4B, 1A, 2B, 2A, 1B, 4A, 1B, 2A, rep from * to end.

Row 9 *K1A, 1B, 2A, 2B, 2A, (1B, 1A) twice, 2B, 2A, 2B, 1A, 1B, rep from * to last 10 sts, 1A, 1B, 2A, 2B, 2A, 1B, 1A.

Row 10 P1B, 8A, 1B, *1A, 8B, 1A, 1B, 8A, 1B, rep from * to end.

Row 11 *K1A, 8B, 1A, 1B, 8A, 1B, rep from * to last 10 sts, 1A, 8B, 1A.

Row 12 P1B, 1A, 2B, 2A, 2B, 1A, 1B, *1A, 1B, 2A, 2B, 2A, (1B, 1A) twice, 2B, 2A, 2B, 1A, 1B, rep from * to end.

Row 13 *K2B, 1A, 4B, 1A, 2B, 2A, 1B, 4A, 1B, 2A, rep from * to last 10 sts, 2B, 1A, 4B, 1A, 2B.

Row 14 P3B, 1A, 2B, 1A, 3B, *3A, 1B, 2A, 1B, 3A, 3B, 1A, 2B, 1A, 3B, rep from * to end.
Row 15 *K1B, 1A, 2B, 2A, 2B, (1A, 1B) twice, 2A, 2B, 2A, 1B, 1A, rep from * to last 10 sts, 1B, 1A, 2B, 2A, 2B, 1A, 1B.
Row 16 P1B, 1A, 2B, 2A, 2B, 1A, 1B, *1A, 1B, 2A, 2B, 2A, (1B, 1A) twice, 2B, 2A, 2B, 1A, 1B, rep from * to end.
Row 17 *K3B, 1A, 2B, 1A, 3B, 3A, 1B, 2A, 1B, 3A, rep from * to last 10 sts, 3B, 1A, 2B, 1A, 3B.
Row 18 P2B, 1A, 4B, 1A, 2B, *2A, 1B, 4A, 1B, 2A, 2B, 1A, 4B, 1A, 2B, rep from * to end.
Row 19 *K1B, 1A, 2B, 2A, 2B, (1A, 1B) twice, 2A, 2B, 2A, 1B, 1A, rep from * to last 10 sts, 1B, 1A, 2B, 2A, 2B, 1A, 1B.
Row 20 P1A, 8B, 1A, *1B, 8A, 1B, 1A, 8B, 1A, rep from * to end.
These 20 rows form the patt.

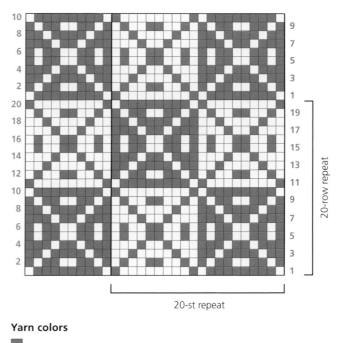

Yarn colors

■ = A
□ = B

variation

This chart shows the blocks aligned to form vertical stripes. Worked on a multiple of 20 stitches.

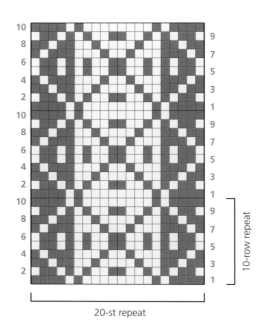

snowflakes and diamonds

This sample shows two pattern repeats. Worked on a multiple of 20 stitches plus 1.

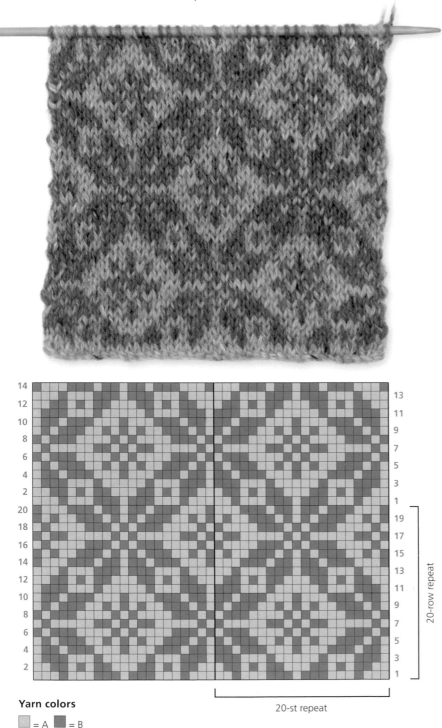

Size 6
(4mm)

Light worsted
weight

Pattern

Row 1 (RS) *K3A, 1B, 3A, 3B, 1A, 3B, 3A, 1B, 2A, rep from * to last st, 1A.
Row 2 P1A, *1A, 2B, 1A, 1B, 1A, 2B, 3A, 2B, 1A, 1B, 1A, 2B, 2A, rep from * to end.
Row 3 *K1A, 3B, 3A, 1B, 5A, 1B, 3A, 3B, rep from * to last st, 1A.
Row 4 P1A, *2B, 1A, 3B, 3A, 1B, 3A, 3B, 1A, 2B, 1A, rep from * to end.
Row 5 *K1A, 1B, 1A, 3B, 2A, 1B, (1A, 1B) twice, 2A, 3B, 1A, 1B, rep from * to last st, 1A.
Row 6 P1B, *1A, 3B, 4A, 1B, 1A, 1B, 4A, 3B, 1A, 1B, rep from * to end.
Row 7 *K1A, 1B, 5A, 2B, 1A, 1B, 1A, 2B, 5A, 1B, rep from * to last st, 1A.
Rows 8 to 13 Rep rows 6 to 1 in this order.
Row 14 P1B, *3A, 3B, 1A, (2B, 1A) twice, 3B, 3A, 1B, rep from * to end.
Row 15 *K1B, 1A, 1B, 2A, 3B, 1A, (1B, 1A) twice, 3B, 2A, 1B, 1A, rep from * to last st, 1B.
Row 16 P1A, *1B, 4A, 3B, 1A, 1B, 1A, 3B, 4A, 1B, 1A, rep from * to end.
Row 17 *K1B, 1A, 2B, 5A, 1B, 1A, 1B, 5A, 2B, 1A, rep from * to last st, 1B.
Row 18 P1A, *1B, 4A, 3B, 1A, 1B, 1A, 3B, 4A, 1B, 1A, rep from * to end.
Row 19 *K1B, 1A, 1B, 2A, 3B, 1A, (1B, 1A) twice, 3B, 2A, 1B, 1A, rep from * to last st, 1B.
Row 20 P1B, *3A, 3B, 1A, (2B, 1A) twice, 3B, 3A, 1B, rep from * to end.
These 20 rows form the patt.

Yarn colors

■ = A   ■ = B

14 12 10 8 6 4 2
20 18 16 14 12 10 8 6 4 2

13 11 9 7 5 3 1
19 17 15 13 11 9 7 5 3 1

20-row repeat

20-st repeat

variation

A third color can be introduced on rows
6 to 8 and 16 to 18 to form a horizontal
stripe across the center of each snowflake.

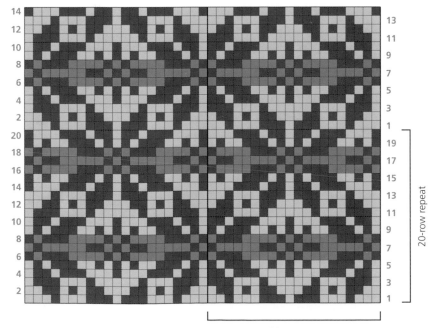

Size 6
(4mm)

Light worsted
weight

zigzag panels

This sample shows three pattern repeats. Worked on a multiple of 12 stitches plus 1.

 Size 6
(4mm)

Light worsted
weight

Pattern

Row 1 (RS) *K2B, 2A, 4B, 2A, 1B, 1A, rep from * to last st, 1B.
Row 2 P1B, *1B, 2A, 1B, 5A, 3B, rep from * to end.
Row 3 *K2B, 2A, 4B, 2A, 1B, 1A, rep from * to last st, 1B.
Row 4 P1B, *2A, 1B, 5A, 1B, 2A, 1B, rep from * to end.
Row 5 *K1B, 1A, 1B, 5A, 1B, 3A, rep from * to last st, 1B.
Row 6 P1B, *4A, 1B, 2A, 1B, (1A, 1B) twice, rep from * to end.
Row 7 *(K1B, 2A) 4 times, rep from * to last st, 1B.
Row 8 P1B, *(1A, 1B) twice, 2A, 1B, 4A, 1B, rep from * to end.
Row 9 *K1B, 3A, 1B, 5A, 1B, 1A, rep from * to last st, 1B.
Row 10 P1B, *2A, 1B, 5A, 1B, 2A, 1B, rep from * to end.
Row 11 *K1B, 1A, 1B, 2A, 4B, 2A, 1B, rep from * to last st, 1B.

Row 12 P1B, *2B, 5A, 1B, 2A, 2B, rep from * to end.
Row 13 *K1B, 1A, 1B, 2A, 4B, 2A, 1B, rep from * to last st, 1B.
Row 14 P1B, *2A, 1B, 5A, 1B, 2A, 1B, rep from * to end.
Row 15 *K1B, 3A, 1B, 5A, 1B, 1A, rep from * to last st, 1B.
Row 16 P1B, *(1A, 1B) twice, 2A, 1B, 4A, 1B, rep from * to end.
Row 17 *(K1B, 2A) 4 times, rep from * to last st, 1B.
Row 18 P1B, *4A, 1B, 2A, 1B, (1A, 1B) twice, rep from * to end.
Row 19 *K1B, 1A, 1B, 5A, 1B, 3A, rep from * to last st, 1B.
Row 20 P1B, *2A, 1B, 5A, 1B, 2A, 1B, rep from * to end.
These 20 rows form the patt.

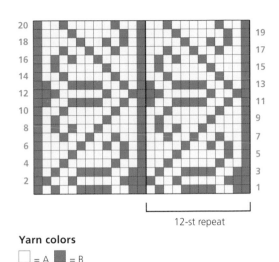

Yarn colors

☐ = A ■ = B

12-st repeat

variation

This chart shows the zigzag pattern as horizontal bands. Worked on a multiple of 20 stitches plus 3.

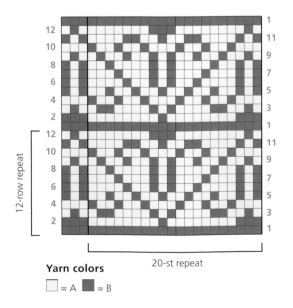

Yarn colors

☐ = A ■ = B

20-st repeat

12-row repeat

Pattern

Row 1 (RS) With B, K to end.
Row 2 P3B, *8A, 1B, 8A, 3B, rep from * to end.
Row 3 *K1A, 1B, 2A, 2B, 4A, 1B, 1A, 1B, 4A, 2B, 1A, rep from * to last 3 sts, 1A, 1B, 1A.
Row 4 P3A, *1B, (2A, 1B) twice, 3A, 1B, (2A, 1B) twice, 3A, rep from * to end.
Row 5 *K1B, 1A, (1B, 2A) 6 times, rep from * to last 3 sts, 1B, 1A, 1B.
Row 6 P1B, 1A, 1B, *4A, 1B, 2A, 1B, 1A, 1B, 2A, 1B, 4A, 1B, 1A, 1B, rep from * to end.
Row 7 *K1B, 1A, 1B, (3A, 1B) twice, 1A, (1B, 3A) twice, rep from * to last 3 sts, 1B, 1A, 1B.
Row 8 P1B, 1A, 1B, *2A, 1B, 4A, 1B, 1A, 1B, 4A, 1B, 2A, 1B, 1A, 1B, rep from * to end.
Row 9 *K1A, (1B, 2A) 3 times, 1B, 1A, 1B, (2A, 1B) twice, 1A, rep from * to last 3 sts, 1A, 1B, 1A.
Row 10 P3A, *1B, (2A, 1B) twice, 3A, 1B, (2A, 1B) twice, 3A, rep from * to end.
Row 11 *K1B, 1A, 1B, 4A, 2B, 2A, 1B, 2A, 2B, 4A, rep from * to last 3 sts, 1B, 1A, 1B.
Row 12 P1A, 1B, 1A, *7A, 3B, 8A, 1B, 1A, rep from * to end.
These 12 rows form the patt.

diamonds and crosses

This sample shows one pattern repeat. Worked on a multiple of 22 stitches plus 13.

Size 8
(5mm)

Worsted
weight

Pattern

Row 1 (RS) *K1B, (2A, 1B) 4 times, 1A, (1B, 1A) 4 times, rep from * to last 13 sts, 1B, (2A, 1B) 4 times.

Row 2 P1A, (1B, 1A) 6 times, *1A, 1B, (2A, 1B) 3 times, 1A, (1B, 1A) 5 times, rep from * to end.

Row 3 *K3A, 1B, (1A, 1B) 3 times, 3A, 1B, 2A, 1B, 1A, 1B, 2A, 1B, rep from * to last 13 sts, 3A, 1B, (1A, 1B) 3 times, 3A.

Row 4 P4B, 1A, (1B, 1A) twice, 4B, *2A, 1B, 3A, 1B, 2A, 4B, 1A, (1B, 1A) twice, 4B, rep from * to end.

Row 5 *K5A, 1B, 1A, 1B, 6A, 1B, (2A, 1B) twice, 1A, rep from * to last 13 sts, 5A, 1B, 1A, 1B, 5A.

Row 6 P1A, 4B, 1A, 1B, 1A, 4B, 1A, *1B, 2A, 3B, 2A, 1B, 1A, 4B, 1A, 1B, 1A, 4B, 1A, rep from * to end.

Row 7 *K1B, 4A, 3B, 4A, 1B, 2A, 2B, 1A, 2B, 2A, rep from * to last 13 sts, 1B, 4A, 3B, 4A, 1B.

Rows 8 to 13 Rep rows 6 to 1 in this order.

Row 14 (P2A, 1B) twice, 1A, (1B, 2A) twice, *(1A, 1B) 4 times, 3A, 1B, 2A, 1B, 1A, (1B, 2A) twice, rep from * to end.

Row 15 *K2B, 2A, 1B, 3A, 1B, 2A, 4B, 1A, (1B, 1A) twice, 2B, rep from * to last 13 sts, 2B, 2A, 1B, 3A, 1B, 2A, 2B.

Row 16 P3A, 1B, (2A, 1B) twice, 3A, *3A, 1B, 1A, 1B, 6A, 1B, (2A, 1B) twice, 3A, rep from * to end.

Row 17 *K1B, 1A, 1B, 2A, 3B, 2A, 1B, 1A, 4B, 1A, 1B, 1A, 3B, rep from * to last 13 sts, 1B, 1A, 1B, 2A, 3B, 2A, 1B, 1A, 1B.

Row 18 P1A, 1B, 2A, 2B, 1A, 2B, 2A, 1B, 1A, *3A, 3B, 4A, 1B, 2A, 2B, 1A, 2B, 2A, 1B, 1A, rep from * to end.

Rows 19 to 22 Rep rows 17 to 14 in this order.

These 22 rows form the patt.

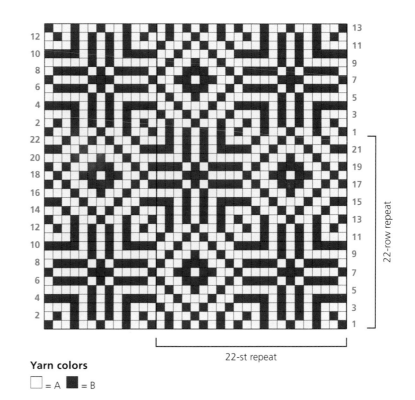

Yarn colors

☐ = A ■ = B

variation

A third color can be introduced on rows 5 to 9 and 16 to 20 to form horizontal stripes in the pattern.

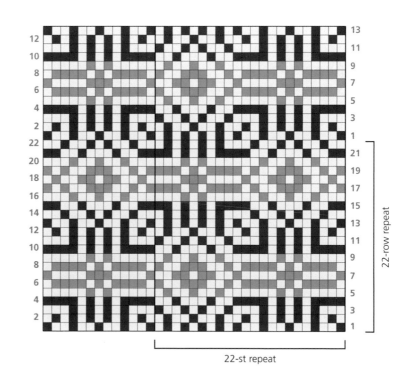

diamonds and snowflakes

This sample shows two pattern
repeats. Worked on a multiple
of 24 stitches plus 1.

 Size 5
(3.75mm)

Light worsted
weight

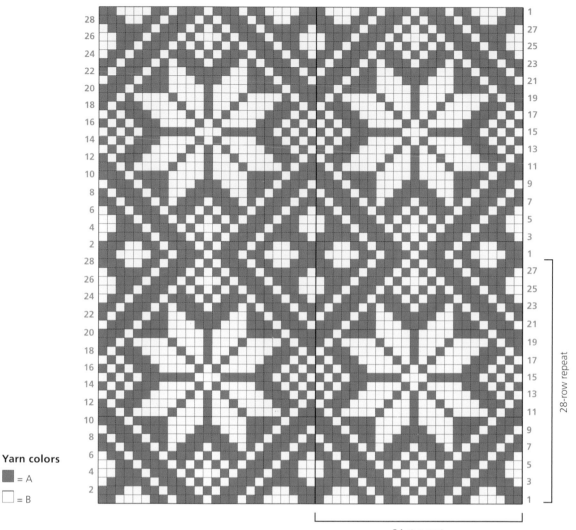

28-row repeat

24-st repeat

Yarn colors

■ = A

□ = B

Pattern

Row 1 (RS) *K2A, 4B, 2A, 1B, (3A, 1B) twice, 2A, 4B, 1A, rep from * to last st, 1A.
Row 2 P1A, *2A, 2B, 2A, 1B, 3A, 1B, 1A, 1B, 3A, 1B, 2A, 2B, 3A, rep from * to end.
Row 3 *K1B, 5A, 1B, 3A, 1B, (1A, 1B) twice, 3A, 1B, 5A, rep from * to last st, 1B.
Row 4 P1B, *1B, (3A, 1B) twice, 1A, 3B, 1A, (1B, 3A) twice, 2B, rep from * to end.
Row 5 *K2B, 2A, 1B, 3A, 1B, (1A, 1B) 4 times, 3A, 1B, 2A, 1B, rep from * to last st, 1B.
Row 6 P1B, *2A, 1B, (3A, 1B) twice, 1A, 1B, (3A, 1B) twice, 2A, 1B, rep from * to end.

Row 7 *K2A, 1B, 3A, 1B, 1A, 1B, (3A, 1B) twice, 1A, 1B, 3A, 1B, 1A, rep from * to last st, 1A.
Row 8 P1A, *1B, 3A, 1B, 2A, 2B, 5A, 2B, 2A, 1B, 3A, 1B, 1A, rep from * to end.
Row 9 *(K1B, 3A) twice, (3B, 3A) twice, 1B, 3A, rep from * to last st, 1B.
Row 10 P1A, *2A, 1B, 4A, 4B, 1A, 4B, 4A, 1B, 3A, rep from * to end.
Row 11 *K2A, 1B, 1A, 4B, 1A, (3B, 1A) twice, 4B, 1A, 1B, 1A, rep from * to last st, 1A.

Row 12 P1A, *1B, 3A, 4B, 1A, (2B, 1A) twice, 4B, 3A, 1B, 1A, rep from * to end.
Row 13 *K1B, 1A, 1B, 3A, 4B, 1A, (1B, 1A) twice, 4B, 3A, 1B, 1A, rep from * to last st, 1B.
Row 14 P1A, *1B, 1A, 1B, 3A, 4B, 1A, 1B, 1A, 4B, 3A, (1B, 1A) twice, rep from * to end.
Row 15 *K1B, (1A, 1B) twice, 6A, 3B, 6A, (1B, 1A) twice, rep from * to last st, 1B.
Rows 16 to 28 Rep rows 14 to 2 in this order.
These 28 rows form the patt.

leaves and blocks

This sample shows two pattern
repeats. Worked on a multiple
of 28 stitches plus 1.

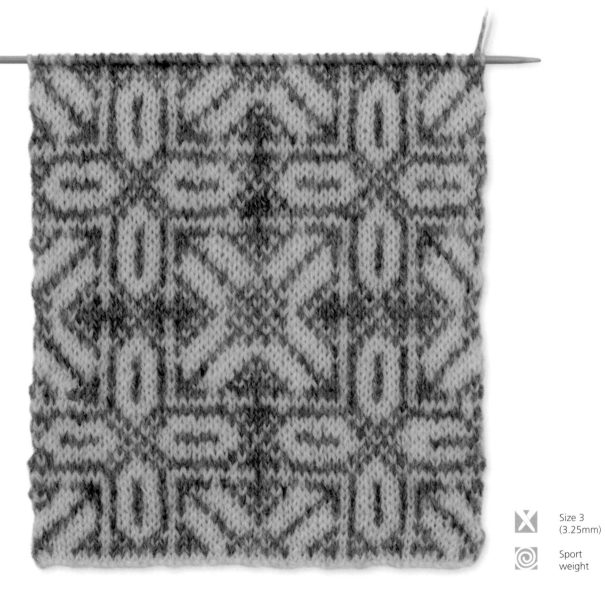

Size 3
(3.25mm)

Sport
weight

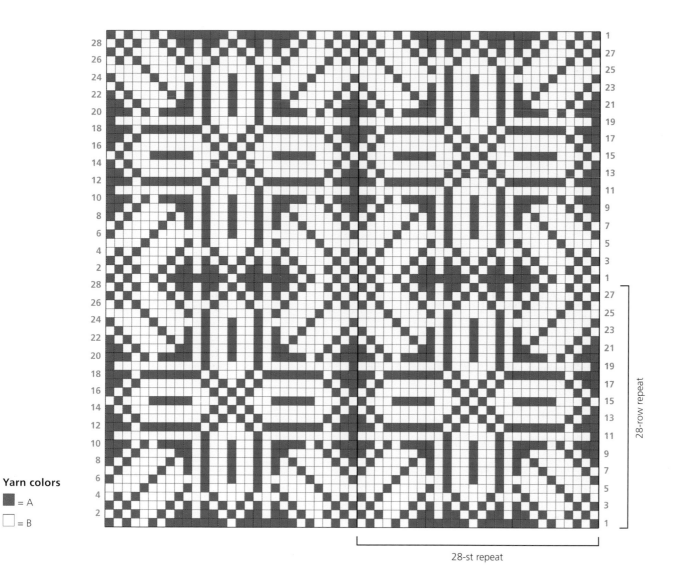

28-row repeat

28-st repeat

Yarn colors

■ = A

□ = B

Pattern

Row 1 (RS) *K1A, 1B, 1A, 2B, 1A, 1B, (7A, 1B) twice, 1A, 2B, 1A, 1B, rep from * to last st, 1A.

Row 2 P1B, *1A, 1B, 1A, 2B, 1A, (1B, 2A) twice, 1B, 1A, 1B, (2A, 1B) twice, 1A, 2B, (1A, 1B) twice, rep from * to end.

Row 3 *K1A, 1B, 1A, 4B, 1A, (1B, 1A) 7 times, 4B, 1A, 1B, rep from * to last st, 1A.

Row 4 P1B, *1A, 1B, 1A, 4B, 1A, (3B, 1A) 3 times, 4B, (1A, 1B) twice, rep from * to end.

Row 5 *(K4B, 1A) twice, 1B, 1A, 5B, 1A, 1B, 1A, 4B, 1A, 3B, rep from * to last st, 1B.

Row 6 P1A, *4B, 1A, 5B, 1A, (2B, 1A) twice, 5B, 1A, 4B, rep from * to end.

Row 7 *K1B, 1A, 4B, 1A, 2B, 1A, 1B, 1A, (2B, 1A) twice, 1B, 1A, 2B, 1A, 4B, 1A, rep from * to last st, 1B.

Row 8 P1A, *1B, 1A, 4B, 1A, (1B, 1A) twice, (2B, 1A) twice, (1B, 1A) twice, 4B, 1A, 1B, 1A, rep from * to end.

Row 9 *K2A, 1B, 1A, 4B, 2A, 1B, 1A, (2B, 1A) twice, 1B, 2A, 4B, 1A, 1B, 1A, rep from * to last st, 1A.

Row 10 P1A, *2A, 1B, 1A, 1B, 4A, 1B, 1A, (2B, 1A) twice, 1B, 4A, 1B, 1A, 1B, 3A, rep from * to end.

Row 11 *K1A, 10B, 1A, 5B, 1A, 10B, rep from * to last st, 1A.

Row 12 P1A, *2A, 1B, 7A, 1B, 1A, 3B, 1A, 1B, 7A, 1B, 3A, rep from * to end.

Row 13 *K2A, 1B, 1A, 7B, 1A, (1B, 1A) 3 times, 7B, 1A, 1B, 1A, rep from * to last st, 1A.

Row 14 P1A, *1B, 1A, 9B, 1A, (1B, 1A) twice, 9B, 1A, 1B, 1A, rep from * to end.

Row 15 *K1B, 1A, 3B, 5A, 3B, 1A, 1B, 1A, 3B, 5A, 3B, 1A, rep from * to last st, 1B.

Rows 16 to 28 Rep rows 14 to 2 in this order.

These 28 rows form the patt.

arrowheads

This sample shows one pattern repeat. Worked on a multiple of 51 stitches plus 1.

X Size 3 (3.25mm)

Sport weight

Pattern

Row 1 (RS) *K1B, 8A, 5B, 3A, 2B, (6A, 2B) twice, 3A, 5B, 8A, rep from * to last st, 1B.
Row 2 P1A, *5B, 4A, 3B, 3A, 2B, 2A, (5B, 2A) twice, 2B, 3A, 3B, 4A, 5B, 1A, rep from * end.
Row 3 *K1A, 1B, 1A, 4B, 4A, 1B, 3A, 2B, 2A, 4B, 1A, 1B, 2A, 1B, 1A, 4B, 2A, 2B, 3A, 1B, 4A, 4B, 1A, 1B, rep from * to last st, 1A.
Row 4 P1A, *2B, 1A, 4B, 6A, 2B, 2A, 4B, 1A, 2B, 2A, 2B, 1A, 4B, 2A, 2B, 6A, 4B, 1A, 2B, 1A, rep from * to end.
Row 5 *K1A, 3B, 1A, 4B, 4A, 2B, 2A, 4B, 1A, 3B, 2A, 3B, 1A, 4B, 2A, 2B, 4A, 4B, 1A,

3B, rep from * to last st, 1A.
Row 6 P1A, *9B, 2A, 2B, 2A, (9B, 2A) twice, 2B, 2A, 9B, 1A, rep from * to end.
Row 7 *K2A, 7B, 2A, 2B, (4A, 7B) twice, 4A, 2B, 2A, 7B, 1A, rep from * to last st, 1A.
Row 8 P1A, *2A, 4B, 3A, 2B, 7A, 4B, 2A, 2B, 2A, 4B, 7A, 2B, 3A, 4B, 3A, rep from * to end.
Row 9 *K4A, 3B, 2A, 2B, 3A, 1B, 2A, 1B, 1A, 3B, 2A, 4B, 2A, 3B, 1A, 1B, 2A, 1B, 3A, 2B, 2A, 3B, 3A, rep from * to last st, 1A.
Row 10 P1B, *4A, 1B, 2A, 2B, 4A, 1B, 1A, 1B, 3A, 1B, 2A, (2B, 2A) twice, 1B, 3A, 1B,

1A, 1B, 4A, 2B, 2A, 1B, 4A, 1B, rep from * to end.
Row 11 *K2B, 5A, 2B, 6A, 1B, 6A, 2B, 4A, 2B, 6A, 1B, 6A, 2B, 5A, 1B, rep from * to last st, 1B.
Row 12 P1B, *2B, 3A, 2B, 3A, 4B, 1A, 2B, 3A, 2B, 6A, 2B, 3A, 2B, 1A, 4B, 3A, 2B, 3A, 3B, rep from * to end.
Row 13 *K2B, 3A, 2B, 4A, 1B, 2A, 1B, 5A, 2B, (3A, 2B) twice, 5A, 1B, 2A, 1B, 4A, 2B, 3A, 1B, rep from * to last st, 1B.
Row 14 P1B, *3A, 2B, 5A, 1B, 2A, 1B, 4A, 2B, 3A, 4B, 3A, 2B, 4A, 1B, 2A, 1B, 5A, 2B,

Yarn colors

☐ = A

■ = B

51-st repeat

3A, 1B, rep from * to end.
Row 15 *(K3A, 2B) twice, 1A, 4B, 3A, 2B,
3A, 6B, 3A, 2B, 3A, 4B, 1A, 2B, 3A, 2B, 2A,
rep from * to last st, 1A.
Row 16 P1A, *1A, 2B, 6A,1B, 6A, 2B, 5A,
4B, 5A, 2B, 6A, 1B, 6A, 2B, 2A, rep from *
to end.
Row 17 *K1A, 2B, 2A, 1B, 3A, 1B, 1A, 1B,
4A, 2B, 2A, 1B, 4A, 2B, 4A, 1B, 2A, 2B, 4A,
1B, 1A, 1B, 3A, 1B, 2A, 2B, rep from * to
last st, 1A.
Row 18 P1B, *1B, 2A, 3B, 1A, 1B, 2A, 1B,
3A, 2B, 2A, 3B, 8A, 3B, 2A, 2B, 3A, 1B, 2A,
1B, 1A, 3B, 2A, 2B, rep from * to end.

Row 19 *K1B, 2A, 4B, 7A, 2B, 3A, 4B, 6A,
4B, 3A, 2B, 7A, 4B, 2A, rep from * to last
st, 1B.
Row 20 P1A, *1A, 7B, 4A, 2B, 2A, 7B, 4A,
7B, 2A, 2B, 4A, 7B, 2A, rep from * to end.
Row 21 *K1A, 9B, 2A, 2B, 2A, (9B, 2A)
twice, 2B, 2A, 9B, rep from * to last st, 1A.
Row 22 P1A, *3B, 1A, 4B, 2A, 2B, 4A, 4B,
1A, 3B, 2A, 3B, 1A, 4B, 4A, 2B, 2A, 4B, 1A,
3B, 1A, rep from * to end.
Row 23 *K1A, 2B, 1A, 4B, 2A, 2B, 6A, 4B,
1A, 2B, 2A, 2B, 1A, 4B, 6A, 2B, 2A, 4B, 1A,
2B, rep from * to last st, 1A.
Row 24 P1A, *1B, 1A, 4B, 2A, 2B, 3A, 1B,

4A, 4B, 1A, 1B, 2A, 1B, 1A, 4B, 4A, 1B, 3A,
2B, 2A, 4B, 1A, 1B, 1A, rep from * to end.
Row 25 *K1A, 5B, 2A, 2B, 3A, 3B, 4A, 5B,
2A, 5B, 4A, 3B, 3A, 2B, 2A, 5B, rep from *
to last st, 1A.
Row 26 P1B, *6A, 2B, 3A, 5B, 8A, 2B, 8A,
5B, 3A, 2B, 6A, 1B, rep from * to end.
Rows 27 to 52 Rep rows 26 to 1 in this
order, but read K for P and P for K
throughout.
These 52 rows form the patt.

project 8: mug cozies and pot holder

Team chic mug cozies with a useful pot holder. The pot holder is an ideal starter project to practice your circular knitting.

Pattern—mug cozies

TO MAKE
Using size 3 (3.25mm) needles and A, cast on 71 sts.
Rib row 1 (RS) K1, *P1, K1, rep from * to end.
Rib row 2 P1, *K1, P1, rep from * to end.
Change to size 6 (4mm) needles.
Join on B.
Reading odd numbered (RS) rows from right to left and even numbered (WS) rows from left to right, work in Fair Isle patt with ribbed borders as follows:
Row 1 (RS) With A, rib 7; work row 1 of Fair Isle patt to last 7 sts; with A, rib 7.
Row 2 With A, rib 7; work row 2 of Fair Isle patt to last 7 sts; with A, rib 7.
Cont in patt as set until row 13 has been worked.
Cut off B and cont with A only.
Next row Rib 7, P to last 7 sts, rib 7.
Change to size 3 (3.25mm) needles.
Work the 2 rib rows 3 times.
Bind off knitwise.

Pattern—pot holder

TO MAKE
Using size 6 (4mm) circular needle and B, cast on 98 sts.
Mark the beg of the round.
Join on A.
Reading every row from right to left, work the 16 rows of Fair Isle patt from chart 3 times, then work row 1 again. Bind off with B.

YOU WILL NEED (for the set)
- 50g light worsted weight yarn in main color (A)
- 50g light worsted weight yarn in contrast color (B)
- Size 3 (3.25mm) and size 6 (4mm) knitting needles for mug cozies
- Size 6 (4mm) circular knitting needle for pot holder

SIZE
Mug cozies 10½in (27cm) circumference x 3¼in (8cm) high
To fit mug with circumference of 11½in (29cm) and with bottom of handle at no less than ½in (1cm) above base of mug
Pot holder 7½ x 7½in (19 x 19cm), excluding hanging loop

GAUGE
26 sts and 27 rows to 4in (10cm) over Fair Isle patt

TO FINISH MUG COZIES
Block knitting to size. Weave in the ends, then join top and bottom of side edges to fit handle of mug.

TO FINISH POT HOLDER
Block knitting to size. Weave in the ends, then join top and bottom edges. Using four 1yd (1m) lengths of A, make a twisted cord (see page 136). Tie a flat knot in the cord, forming a 3in (8cm) loop at the center. Sew the loop to the center top edge of the pot holder.

Mug cozies

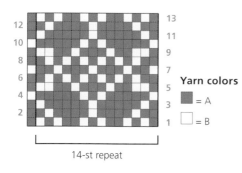

14-st repeat

Yarn colors

■ = A

□ = B

Pot holder

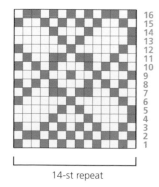

14-st repeat

Yarn colors

■ = A

□ = B

project 9 : bag

This colorful bag is worked in just two yarns—a beautiful space-dyed yarn is used for the background and a solid color for the patterning. Stiffened and finished with leather handles, this bag is sure to appeal.

YOU WILL NEED
- 200g spaced-dyed bulky weight yarn in main color (A)
- 100g worsted weight yarn in contrast color (B)
- Size 8 (5mm) and size 9 (5.5mm) knitting needles
- Lining fabric
- Buckram for stiffening
- Tapestry needle
- Matching stranded embroidery thread
- Pair of 20in (50cm) leather bag handles

SIZE
10¼in wide x 10½in high x 4¾in deep
(26cm wide x 27cm high x 12cm deep)

GAUGE
20 sts and 20 rows to 4in (10cm) over Fair Isle patt

Pattern

BACK AND FRONT (alike)
Using size 9 (5.5mm) needles and A, cast on 73 sts.
Join on B. Reading odd numbered (RS) rows from right to left and even numbered (WS) rows from left to right, work in Fair Isle patt from chart until work measures 13in (33cm) from beg, ending row 1.
Cut off B.
With A, P 2 rows.
Change to size 8 (5mm) needles.
Beg with a P row, work 4 rows st st for facing. Bind off.

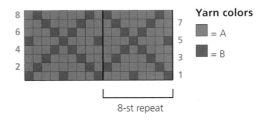

8-st repeat

Yarn colors
= A
= B

TO FINISH
Block knitting to size. Using the knitting as a pattern, cut two rectangles of lining fabric, allowing ⅝in (1.5cm) at each side and lower edge for seams.

Join side seams of bag pieces, then join lower seam. With the bag inside out, form the base of the bag into a rectangle and fold out the corners. Measure 2½in (6cm) from the point and pin a line across the corner. Backstitch along the line. Turn the bag right side out and push out the base of the bag.

Cut two 4¾ x 10¼in (12 x 26cm) rectangles of buckram for the base. Cut a piece of buckram 10¼in (26cm) by the circumference of the bag, plus ⅝in (1.5cm) for overlap. Join the overlap. Put the two rectangles of buckram in the base of the bag, then insert the circle of buckram so the top edge is level with the ridge row. Turn the facing over the top of the buckram and stitch in place. Using a tapestry needle and six strands of embroidery thread, sew the handles centrally to the top of the bag, sewing through both thicknesses.

Make up the lining fabric as for the bag. Trim the seam allowances. Fold ¾in (2cm) (the depth of the knitted facing) at the top to the wrong side and press.

With WS together and seams matching, insert the lining into bag and pin top edge of lining to lower edge of facing. Slipstitch lining to facing.

project 10: throw

Pattern

FAIR ISLE PANEL

Using size 6 (4mm) circular needle and A, cast on 240 sts.
Place a marker on right needle to mark beg of round.
Slipping the marker on every round and joining on and cutting off colors as required, cont in Fair Isle patt as follows:
Reading every row from right to left, work in Fair Isle patt from chart until work measures 12in (30cm) from beg.
Cut off B and C.
With A, K 1 round. Bind off purlwise.

A deep Fair Isle panel is an attractive addition to a fabric throw. Knit it in colors to complement your décor and use it to dress your favorite chair.

YOU WILL NEED
- 100g worsted weight yarn in main color (A)
- 75g worsted weight yarn in contrast color (B)
- 50g worsted weight yarn in contrast color (C)
- Size 6 (4mm) circular knitting needle, 32in (80cm) long
- Fabric for throw
- Needle and matching sewing thread
- Thin cardboard
- Pair of compasses and pencil
- Scissors

SIZE
Knitted panel 19in (48cm) wide x 12in (30cm) deep
Finished throw 19in (48cm) wide x 58in (150cm) long

GAUGE
25 sts and 26 rows to 4in (10cm) over Fair Isle patt

TO FINISH

Block knitting to size. Join the lower edge. Press seam. Cut a piece of fabric 39in (99cm) wide x 48in (122cm) long. With RS together, join the long seam, taking a ¾in (1.5cm) seam allowance. Press seam open. With the seam at the center, join one short edge. Cut diagonally across the corners to reduce any bulk. Turn through to right side and press. Neaten the raw edge.

With the seam at center back, insert ½in (1cm) of the open end of the fabric between the open edges of the knitted panel. Pin, then sew in place.

Using ¾in (2cm) circles of cardboard, make five pompoms in contrast color B and four pompoms in the main color A and contrast color C (see page 135). Sew the pompons evenly along the lower edge, alternating the colors, as shown.

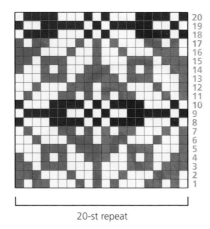

20-st repeat

Yarn colors

 = A

 = B

 = C

project 11: pillows

Pattern—rectangular pillow

FAIR ISLE PANEL
Using size 6 (4mm) needles and C, cast on 42 sts.
Joining on and cutting off colors as required and reading odd numbered (RS) rows from right to left and even numbered (WS) rows from left to right, rep the 20 rows of Fair Isle patt from chart 3 times, then work rows 1 to 10 again. Bind off.

FRONT PANEL
Using size 6 (4mm) needles and A, cast on 51 sts.
Work in basket st as follows:
Row 1 (RS) K3, *P3, K3, rep from * to end.
Row 2 P3, *K3, P3, rep from * to end.
Rows 3 and 4 Rep rows 1 and 2.
Row 5 P3, *K3, P3, rep from * to end.
Row 6 K3, *P3, K3, rep from * to end.
Rows 7 and 8 Rep rows 5 and 6.
These 8 rows form the patt.
Cont in patt until work measures same as Fair Isle panel, ending row 4 or 8. Bind off.

BACK
Using size 6 (4mm) needles and A, cast on 87 sts.
Work as given for front panel.

This pair of striking pillows combines Fair Isle patterns with a basket stitch texture. The rectangular pillow has a Fair Isle panel on the front and the square pillow has a Fair Isle front and textured back.

YOU WILL NEED (rectangular pillow)
• 50g light worsted weight yarn in main color (A)
• 50g light worsted weight yarn in contrast color (B)
• 50g light worsted weight yarn in contrast color (C)
• Size 6 (4mm) knitting needles
• Pillow form

SIZE (rectangular pillow)
16in x 12in (40cm x 30cm)

GAUGE (rectangular pillow)
23 sts and 31 rows to 4in (10cm) over basket st
26 sts and 25 rows to 4in (10cm) over Fair Isle patt

TO FINISH RECTANGULAR PILLOW
Block knitting to size. Join the Fair Isle panel to the front panel. Join back and front together, leaving an opening on one edge to insert the pillow form. Insert the pillow form and sew the opening closed (see designer's tip, left).

designer's tip

Once you have inserted the pillow form, the opening will need to be sewn with the right side facing. You can either slipstitch the opening with small, neat stitches, or if you have been using mattress stitch to join the seams, where you are working on the right side, continue across the opening in the same way.

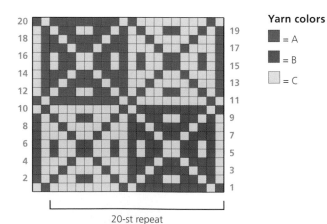

Yarn colors
■ = A
■ = B
□ = C

20-st repeat

designer's tip

Choose a pillow form slightly larger than the size of the pillow cover—this will ensure that you have a nice plump pillow.

Pattern—square pillow

FRONT
Using size 6 (4mm) needles and A, cast on 72 sts.
Joining on and cutting off colors as required and reading odd numbered (RS) rows from right to left and even numbered (WS) rows from left to right, rep the 10 rows of Fair Isle patt from chart 7 times, then work rows 1 and 2 again. Bind off.

BACK
Using size 6 (4mm) needles and A, cast on 63 sts.
Work in basket st as follows:
Row 1 (RS) K3, *P3, K3, rep from * to end.
Row 2 P3, *K3, P3, rep from * to end.
Rows 3 and 4 Rep rows 1 and 2.
Row 5 P3, *K3, P3, rep from * to end.
Row 6 K3, *P3, K3, rep from * to end.
Rows 7 and 8 Rep rows 5 and 6.
These 8 rows form the patt.
Cont in patt until work measures same as front, ending row 4 or 8. Bind off.

YOU WILL NEED (square pillow)
• 100g light worsted weight yarn in main color (A)
• 50g light worsted weight yarn in contrast color (B)
• 50g light worsted weight yarn in contrast color (C)
• Size 6 (4mm) knitting needles
• Pillow form

SIZE (square pillow)
12in (30cm) square

GAUGE (square pillow)
23 sts and 31 rows to 4in (10cm) over basket st
26 sts and 25 rows to 4in (10cm) over Fair Isle patt

TO FINISH SQUARE PILLOW
Block knitting to size. Join back and front together, leaving an opening on one edge to insert the pillow form. Insert the pillow form and sew the opening closed (see designer's tip on page 122).

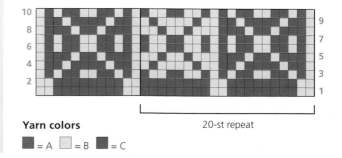

Yarn colors

■ = A □ = B ■ = C

20-st repeat

finishing techniques

Blocking and pressing, mattress stitch, and backstitch—your handknits deserve a perfect finish. Tassels, pompoms, twisted cord, fringing, buttons, and beads—all will enhance your Fair Isle knits with a touch of texture or surface embellishment.

lesson  | blocking and pressing

Before you assemble a project, it is essential to block and/or press all knitted pieces to size and shape. By using heat, water, or steam, you can even out any stitch irregularities and help curled edges lie flat, so giving your knitting a professional finish.

steaming and pressing

Knitting worked in natural fibers, such as wool or cotton, and fairly plain textures can usually be steam-pressed—always check your pattern and the yarn label. Pin the knitted pieces out to size on a blocking board using the grid on the fabric as a guide (see Tip, right), then place a clean dry or damp cloth over the fabric and press lightly with an iron set at the recommended temperature—keep the iron moving and don't leave the full weight of the iron on the fabric. Never place an iron directly on a knitted fabric because you may burn the fibers and spoil the knitting.

Textured fabrics such as seed stitch should not be pressed because this will flatten the pattern. Instead, hold a steam iron over the cloth and allow the steam to pass through to the knitted fabric.

After pressing or steaming, remove the cloth and allow the fabric to dry before removing the knitting from the blocking board.

Ribs can lose their elasticity when pressed, so, unless they need to match the width of the fabric, they are best avoided.

Once the pieces have been joined, the seams will need to be pressed. Working on the wrong side, place a dry or damp cloth over the seams, and use an iron set at the recommended temperature to lightly press the seams.

Do not press or steam synthetic yarns because the heat and steam will take the "body" out of the yarn, making it limp—use the wet or spray method instead.

wet blocking

Use this method for yarn that cannot be pressed, textured yarns, and boldly textured stitch patterns. Wet the knitted sections gently by hand in lukewarm water. Carefully lift the knitting out of the water, gently squeezing out the water as you lift—do not lift it out while it is soaking wet because the weight of the water will stretch the knitting. To remove the excess water, lay the knitting on a towel and smooth out flat, then loosely roll up the towel from one end, applying a little pressure.

Unroll the towel and lay the knitting on a blocking board, or for larger pieces on a towel on a flat surface, such as a worktop or floor. Using long, rustproof glass-headed or knitting pins, pin the knitting out to size and shape. Allow to dry thoroughly to "set" the fabric.

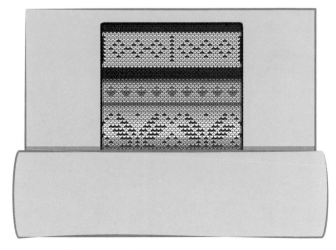

Loosely roll up the towel, applying a little pressure, to remove excess water.

spray blocking

This method is similar to wet blocking and can also be used for yarns that cannot be pressed. Pin out the sections of dry knitting to size and shape on a blocking board, then use a water spray to wet the knitting thoroughly. Press gently with your hands to even out the fabric, then allow to dry before removing the pins.

three-dimensional blocking

For projects worked in the round, use steaming, wet blocking, or spray blocking—choose the method most suited to the yarn and stitch pattern. Work on one side at a time, pinning the knitting out to size, taking care not to damage the stitches. Allow to dry, then repeat on the other side.

If you are blocking a small, circular item such as a hat, you can drape the piece over an upturned plastic pot or mixing bowl that is the right size. Wet the knitting, drape it over the form, and allow to dry.

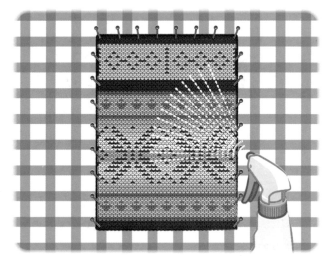

Use a water spray to wet the knitting thoroughly, then allow to dry completely.

A hat can be blocked over a bowl to create a perfect shape.

lesson 21

perfect seams

A beautifully knitted item can be ruined by poor seams. Follow these techniques and you can be assured of a professional finish every time. Refer to the finishing instructions on your pattern for the order of joining the pieces and, unless otherwise stated, use mattress stitch to join the seams.

Tip

Weave in the ends of yarn on each piece of fabric before joining the seams.

mattress stitch

Mattress stitch produces an invisible seam and is worked on the right side of the knitting, making it easy to see how stitches and patterns are aligning.

1 Place the two pieces to be joined side by side with the right sides uppermost and thread the end of yarn from the cast on onto a tapestry needle. To start the seam, insert the needle from back to front through the corner stitch of the opposite piece.

2 Make a figure eight and insert the needle from back to front into the stitch that the end of yarn comes from. Pull the yarn through, and close the gap between the pieces of knitting.

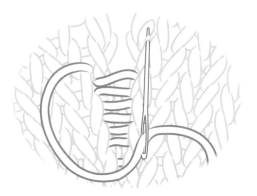

3 Now insert the needle under the horizontal bar between the first and second stitches on the first piece, then under the horizontal bar between the first and second stitches on the second piece. Continue to work backward and forward between the pieces until a few rows have been worked.

4 Draw up the thread to form the seam—do not draw up too tightly or you will distort the fabric. Continue to join the seam in this way. When you reach the end, fasten off neatly by working a few stitches on the wrong side.

backstitch

Backstitch, one of the most commonly used stitches, can also be used to join seams. This is worked with the right sides of the knitting together and the wrong side facing you. To reduce bulk on the seams and to ensure a neat finish, work the stitches near the edge of the knitting.

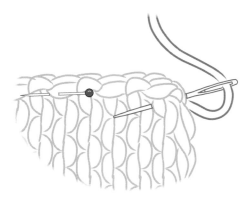

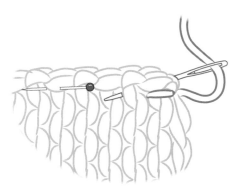

1 Pin the pieces to be joined with the right sides together and the edges level. Thread a tapestry needle with a length of yarn and work a couple of small stitches on the right-hand edge of the back piece of knitting to secure the yarn. Working one stitch in from the edge, insert the needle between the first two rows of knitting from back to front.

2 Take the needle back over the first row, insert it between the first row and the edge, and pull the yarn through. Now insert the needle between the second and third rows and bring to the front, drawing the yarn through.

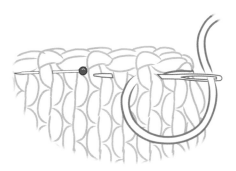

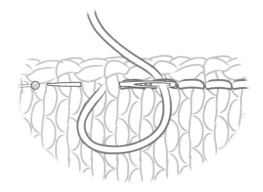

3 Take the needle back over the last row and insert it at the point where the last stitch was worked. Then bring it to the front between the next two rows, and pull the yarn through.

4 Continue to work in this way, inserting the needle at the point where the last stitch was worked from front to back, then inserting it between the next two rows from back to front. At the end of the seam, work a couple of small stitches to secure the yarn. Cut off the yarn.

lesson 22 | adding beads

Decorative beads add a new dimension to Fair Isle knits. When using beads, choose carefully, matching them to the weight and type of yarn—too small and they will disappear into the fabric; too heavy and they will make the knitting sag. Depending on your project, you may need to use washable beads.

sewing on beads

Single beads can be scattered over the right side of a knitted piece to add decoration and texture once the design is complete.

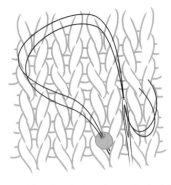

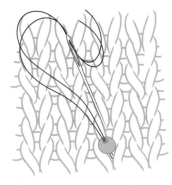

1 Mark the position for the beads on the knitting with pins. Thread a beading needle with a double length of sewing thread and secure it to the wrong side of the knitting, at the position for the first bead, with a few tiny backstitches. Bring the needle to the right side of the work, and thread a bead onto the needle.

2 Take a small stitch through the knitting. Pull the thread through until the bead is sitting on the knitted fabric. Bring the needle through to the front again, through the bead, and back through the knitting to secure the bead. Work a few tiny backstitches on the wrong side and fasten off. Continue to sew on beads in this way.

threading beads onto yarn

These beads should have a hole large enough to let the bead move easily along the yarn—if the hole is too small, it may fray the yarn.

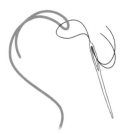

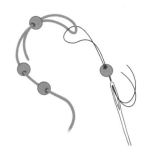

1 Cut a length of sewing thread and fold it in half. Thread the ends through the eye of a needle. Place the end of the knitting yarn through the loop of the thread.

2 Thread on a bead, pushing it along the sewing thread and onto the knitting yarn. Thread on beads in this way until the number of beads required for your project are on the knitting yarn. Remove the yarn from the loop of thread.

knitting in beads

Sections of Fair Isle designs can be emphasized by adding colorful beads within rows of the pattern.

1 On a knit row, knit to the position of the bead, bring the yarn to the front of the work between the needles, and slip the next stitch purlwise.

2 Push a bead along the yarn until it is up against the right-hand needle. Take the yarn to the back of the work and knit the next stitch. Continue to place beads in this way as required.

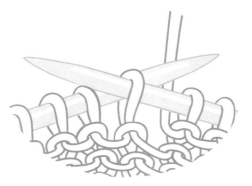

3 On a purl row, purl to the position of the bead, take the yarn to the back between the needles, and slip the next stitch purlwise.

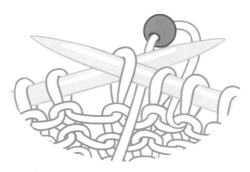

4 Push a bead along the yarn so that it sits behind the slipped stitch. Bring the yarn to the front of the work and purl the next stitch. Continue to place beads in this way as required.

Tip

It is not always possible to thread beads directly onto the yarn, because the bead's hole may be too small to take a needle threaded with yarn. If this is the case, use a length of sewing thread—a leader thread—to thread the beads onto the yarn.

Emphasize sections of Fair Isle patterns with beads.

lesson 23

tassels

Tassels are an ideal trimming for garments and soft furnishings. Made in beautiful yarns such as wool, cotton, tape, or ribbon, they can add a touch of elegance or, in unusual materials such as raffia, leather, or torn fabric, a touch of frivolity.

making tassels

To make a simple tassel you will need yarn or cotton, cardboard, a tapestry needle, and sharp scissors.

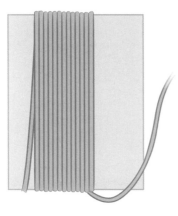

1 Cut a piece of cardboard the required length of the tassel and about 3in (8cm) wide. Hold the cardboard lengthwise in one hand and hold the end of the yarn level with the bottom edge. Now wrap the yarn evenly around the cardboard to the thickness required, finishing at the bottom edge. Cut off the yarn.

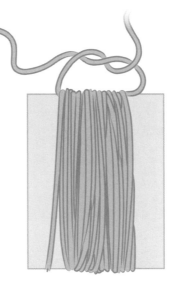

2 Thread a length of yarn onto the tapestry needle and slip the needle under the loops along the top edge. Remove the needle and tie the ends, gathering the loops on the cardboard loosely together. Do not trim the ends because they can be used to attach the tassel.

3 Cut a long length of yarn. Carefully ease the loops off the cardboard and hold them together. Knot one end of the length of yarn around the tassel about a third down from the top. Then wrap the yarn firmly around the tassel as many times as required to cover the knot.

4 Thread the end of the yarn onto the tapestry needle and take it up through the center of the tassel to hide it. Use sharp scissors to cut through the loops at the bottom of the tassel, and to trim the ends.

lesson 24

pompoms

Pompoms are so simple to make and are perfect for trimming throws, pillows, hats, bags, and much more. You can make single-color pompoms or add in extra yarn colors for multicolored variations—just make sure that you cover the cardboard well.

making pompoms

To make a pompom you will need yarn, a pair of compasses, a pencil, cardboard, and sharp scissors.

1 On the cardboard, use a pencil and a pair of compasses to draw a circle the size of the pompom. Now draw another circle inside it, about a third of the diameter of the first circle. Use the scissors to cut around the pencil lines of the two circles, so forming a ring. Make a second ring in the same way.

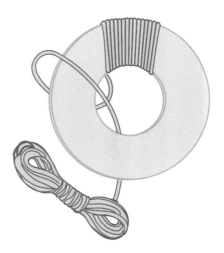

2 With the two rings together, wind yarn evenly around them—don't pull the yarn too tight. Continue to wind yarn until the center hole is filled.

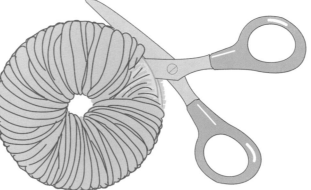

3 To form the pompom, insert a scissor blade between the cardboard rings and cut the yarn around the outer edges. Slip a length of yarn between the rings and tie it tightly. Pull or tear off the cardboard and fluff out the pompom. Trim any uneven ends, but leave the yarn tie for attaching the pompom to your work.

lesson 25

twisted cord

It's easy to make your own cords to use as ties, edgings, and trims. You can use almost any kind of yarn—from fine mohair to chunky wool, or even leather thong or string. Either match the cord to the knitted fabric or go for a complete contrast. Alternatively, combine strands of yarn in different colors or textures for a dramatic or subtle effect.

Tip

Twisted cord requires long lengths of yarn—they should be three times the required finished length of the cord. Decide how thick you want your finished cord to be, then knot together enough lengths to make half that thickness.

making a twisted cord

To make a twisted cord you will need yarn, a tape measure, a wooden board, drawing pins (optional), and sharp scissors.

1 Cut lengths of yarn three times the required length of the cord and knot them together at one end. Pin the knotted ends to a wooden board using a drawing pin. Alternatively, tie the ends to a door handle or sturdy hook to secure.

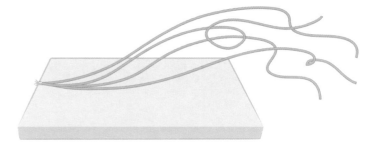

2 Tie the loose ends around a pencil. Pull the yarn out straight and turn the pencil in one direction until the lengths of yarn are firmly twisted. Keep the yarn fairly taut to ensure that the twists are even.

Tip

If you are using the cord as a tie, knot the ends of the cord, then use sharp scissors to trim the ends. Untwist the yarn ends to form a small tassel.

3 Fold the twisted yarn lengths in half and allow the strands to twist around each other. Run your hand down the cord to even out the twists. Holding the ends securely, release them and knot together to secure. Trim the ends.

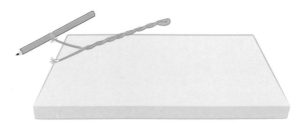

lesson  | fringing

Fringing is a very versatile trim, adding a dramatic finish to plain edges—particularly on throws, wraps, scarves, and pillow flaps. You can work a fringe in one color or texture, or add in extra yarn colors or a variety of textures for added impact.

making a simple fringe

To make a simple fringe you will need yarn, stiff cardboard, sharp scissors, and a crochet hook or hairpin.

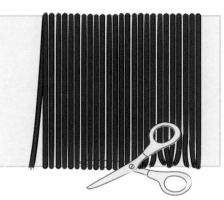

1 Cut a piece of cardboard the required length of the fringe plus 1in (2.5cm) and about 6in (15cm) wide. Hold the cardboard in one hand and hold the end of the yarn level with the bottom edge. Wrap the yarn evenly around the cardboard, taking the yarn over both sides for each single strand of fringing.

2 Using a sharp pair of scissors, cut the loops along the bottom edge and lay the strands out flat. Repeat this process to make more fringing if required.

3 Take the number of strands desired and fold them in half, forming a loop. Insert a crochet hook or hairpin through the edge of the knitting from back to front, catch the loop of fringing, and draw it through the knitting.

4 Use the crochet hook or hairpin to draw the ends of the strands through the loop. Pull the ends carefully to draw the knot up close to the edge. Repeat along the edge.

5 Place the fringe on a flat surface and lay the ends straight. Use sharp scissors to trim the ends evenly.

lesson 27 | adding buttons

Buttons can be used as simple fastenings or to add a decorative touch. There are so many beautiful buttons available that you will be spoiled for choice. Plan out the position of the buttons before you start securing them in place.

Tip

If you are using buttons and buttonholes as a fastening, make sure the button is the right size for the buttonhole—too small and it will keep coming undone; too big and you will stretch the hole. Always start by marking the button positions, as stated in the "Finishing" section of the pattern.

buttons with two holes

This style of button can be attached with the holes positioned horizontally, as shown, or vertically. They also lend themselves to decorative finishes.

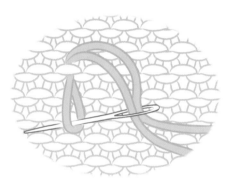

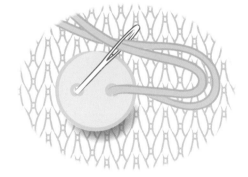

1 Cut a length of yarn or thread, fold it in half, and thread the ends through a large-eyed needle. Working on the wrong side of the knitting, insert the needle through the knitting in the marked button position. Pull the ends of the yarn through, then insert the needle through the loop and draw up to secure.

2 Insert the needle from back to front through the knitting, then up through one hole of the button. Take the needle down through the other hole and through the knitting from front to back. Repeat as many times as required, then work a few small stitches on the wrong side to secure.

Beaded straight stitch

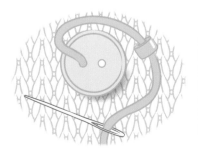

1 Thread a length of yarn or thread through a needle and work a few small stitches on the back of the knitting in the marked button position to secure. Insert the needle from back to front, up through the knitting and one hole of the button. Now insert the needle through a small bead.

2 Take the needle down through the other hole of the button from front to back. Repeat once more, then work a few small stitches on the wrong side to secure.

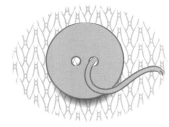
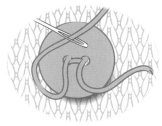

Tied

1 Cut a length of yarn and thread one end through a large-eyed needle. Working on the right side, take the needle down through one hole of the button and through the knitting at the marked button position, from front to back, leaving a 2in (5cm) end on the right side.

2 Insert the needle up through the knitting and the second hole of the button, from back to front, then take the needle down through the first hole and back up through the second hole again.

3 Cut off the yarn, leaving a 2in (5cm) end. Now tie a square knot—take the left end over the right and around, then take the right end over the left and around, and pull the ends to secure. Trim the ends as required.

buttons with four holes

Buttons with four holes can be attached using the conventional method—working horizontal or vertical parallel bars—or with a decorative cross stitch, as shown here. Use a contrasting color thread for added interest.

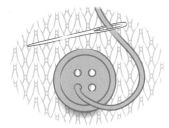
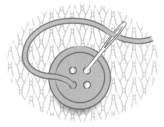

Cross stitch

1 Cut a length of yarn and thread one end through a large-eyed needle. Working on the wrong side of the knitting, sew a few small stitches to secure the yarn at the button position. Now take the needle up through the knitting from back to front, and through one hole of the button.

2 Lay the button in position on the knitting with the thread at the bottom left, and take the needle down through the hole at top right and through the knitting.

3 Bring the needle up through the knitting and through the hole at bottom right, then down through the hole at top left—this forms the first cross. Work another cross in this way, then fasten off by working a few small stitches on the wrong side of the knitting.

lesson 28

aftercare essentials

It is important to take care of your finished knits—designs knitted in a quality yarn will last for many years if washed and cared for properly. Follow these simple guidelines to achieve the best results.

machine washing

Before you wash any item, check the yarn label for washing instructions. For best results use soap flakes, mild detergent, or specially formulated liquids. Many yarns are now machine-washable but do take care to select the correct cycle. To prevent the knitting from shrinking or becoming matted or felted, wash on a delicate wool cycle with as little fast-spin action as possible.

hand washing

When washing your knits by hand, use warm water rather than hot, and make sure that the detergent is completely dissolved before submerging your knits. Handle them gently in the water—do not rub or scrub the knitting or wring it out, because this can felt the fabric. Rinse well to get rid of any soap and squeeze out excess water. Never lift a soaking wet item out of the water or you will stretch the knitting. Instead, gently squeeze out the water as you carefully lift the knitting section by section out of the water. Lay each section lifted out of the water on a surface while you handle the next section.

drying

It is important to remove as much water as possible before laying out the knitting to dry. Lay the item flat on a towel and roll up from one end, applying a little pressure—the towel will absorb excess water.

Lay the damp item flat on a dry towel and smooth it gently to size and pat to shape. Let it dry away from direct heat such as sunlight or a radiator, and turn it occasionally.

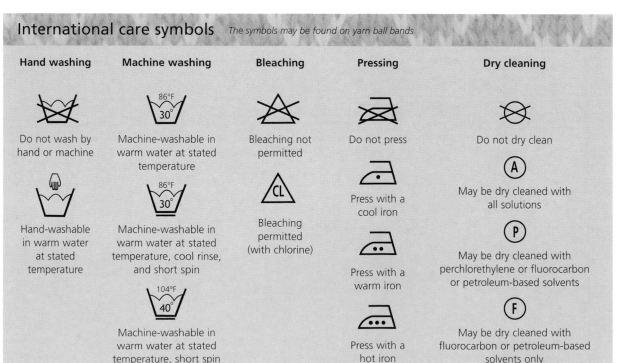

International care symbols *The symbols may be found on yarn ball bands*

Hand washing	Machine washing	Bleaching	Pressing	Dry cleaning
Do not wash by hand or machine	Machine-washable in warm water at stated temperature (86°F 30°)	Bleaching not permitted	Do not press	Do not dry clean
Hand-washable in warm water at stated temperature	Machine-washable in warm water at stated temperature, cool rinse, and short spin (86°F 30°)	Bleaching permitted (with chlorine) (CL)	Press with a cool iron	May be dry cleaned with all solutions (A)
	Machine-washable in warm water at stated temperature, short spin (104°F 40°)		Press with a warm iron	May be dry cleaned with perchlorethylene or fluorocarbon or petroleum-based solvents (P)
			Press with a hot iron	May be dry cleaned with fluorocarbon or petroleum-based solvents only (F)

abbreviations

K
knit

P
purl

st(s)
stitch(es)

st st
stockinette stitch

rev st st
reverse stockinette stitch

g st
garter stitch

sd st
seed stitch

patt
pattern

rep(s)
repeat(s)

cont
continue(ing)

beg
beginning

rem
remain(ing)

alt
alternate

foll
following

tog
together

dec
decrease(ing)

inc
increase(ing)

tbl
through back of loop(s)

yfd
yarn forward

sl
slip

psso
pass slipped stitch over

p2sso
pass 2 slipped stitches over

skpo
sl 1, K1, pass slipped stitch over

ssk
slip the first stitch knitwise, then
slip the second stitch knitwise,
insert the tip of the left-hand
needle through the front loop
of both slipped stitches together,
K the stitches together

puk
pick up loop lying between
needles and K into back of it

pup
pick up loop lying between
needles and P into back of it

RS
right side

WS
wrong side

LH
left hand

RH
right hand

in
inch(es)

mm
millimeter(s)

cm
centimeter(s)

yd
yard(s)

m
meter(s)

Suppliers

Yarn suppliers

Berroco
www.berroco.com

Brown Sheep Company, Inc.
www.brownsheep.com

Cascade Yarns
www.cascadeyarns.com

Classic Elite Yarns
www.classiceliteyarns.com

Coats & Clark
www.coatsandclark.com

Debbie Bliss
www.debbieblissonline.com

Lion Brand Yarn
www.lionbrand.com

Patons Yarn
www.patonsyarns.com

Rowan
www.knitrowan.com

Other useful resources:

Michael's
www.michaels.com

JoAnn
www.joann.com

index

Credits

Yarn information

The following Jamieson's Spinning Ltd, Rowan, Debbie Bliss, and Noro yarns have been used for the knitting patterns in this book.

Child's cardigan (Project 1)
Rowan Handknit Cotton 100% Cotton 85m/93yd/50g

Child's hoodie (Project 2)
Debbie Bliss Cotton DK 100% Cotton 84m/92yd/50g

Fingerless mitts (Project 3)
Rowan Kid Classic 70% Lambswool/22% Kid Mohair/8% Polyamide 140m/153yd/50g

Hot water bottle cover (Project 4)
Jamieson's DK 100% Shetland Wool 75m/82yd/25g

Beret (Project 5)
Rowan Colorspun 72% Wool/14% Mohair/14% Polyamide 135m/148yd/50g
Rowan Kid Classic 70% Lambswool/22% Kid Mohair/8% Polyamide 140m/153yd/50g

Leg warmers (Project 6)
Rowan Felted Tweed DK 50% Merino Wool/25% Alpaca/25% Viscose 175m/191yd/50g

Hat and scarf (Project 7)
Rowan Felted Tweed Aran 50% Merino Wool/25% Alpaca/25% Viscose 87m/95yd/50g

Mug cozies and pot holder (Project 8)
Jamieson's DK 100% Shetland Wool 75m/82yd/25g

Bag (Project 9)
Noro Kochoran 50% Wool/30% Angora/20% Silk 160m/174yd/100g
Debbie Bliss Rialto Aran 100% Merino Wool 80m/87yd/50g

Throw (Project 10)
Jamieson's DK 100% Shetland Wool 75m/82yd/25g

Pillows (Project 11)
Rowan Felted Tweed DK 50% Merino Wool/25% Alpaca/25% Viscose 175m/191yd/50g

Go to the websites below to find a mail order stockist or store in your area:
www.knitrowan.com
www.debbleblissonline.com
www.jamiesonsofshetland.co.uk
www.eisakunoro.com

Acknowledgments

I would like to thank the following people for their invaluable contribution in helping me to create this book:

Kate Kirby and Moira Clinch—it's been a pleasure working with you again. Chloe Todd Fordham for her editing skills. Caroline Guest and Tanya Goldsmith for their creative design. Phil Wilkins for the clarity shown in photography of the stitch patterns and the wonderful chapter openers. Lizzie Orme for photographing the projects so beautifully. Kuo Kang Chen for the technical charts. Marilyn Wilson for her thorough pattern checking. Special thanks to Jamieson's and Rowan for their generosity in supplying gorgeous yarns for some of the projects. What a team!